The Woman's Book of Dirty Words

A *Not Ready for Granny Panties* Book

by Mary Fran Bontempo

© 2015 Mary Fran Bontempo

Illustrations © 2015 Pat Achilles

All rights reserved.

Published by eBookIt.com

ISBN-13: 978-1-4566-2538-2

No part of this book may be reproduced in any form or by any electronic or mechanical means including information storage and retrieval systems, without permission in writing from the author. The only exception is by a reviewer, who may quote short excerpts in a review.

Praise for Mary Fran Bontempo's
The Woman's Book of Dirty Words

"As an editor and publisher, and an internationally syndicated columnist and journalist prior to WVM, words are a part of my everyday life. 'Words' usually mean 'work' to me. But, having read Mary Fran Bontempo's earlier book, I was delighted to read her new book *The Woman's Book of Dirty Words* just for fun. Mary Fran had me smiling from the first chapter to genuinely laughing out loud in many areas, while nodding my head in agreement with the familiar, hilarious life observations she is a master at illuminating. As always, Mary Fran's take on life is highly relatable and relevant for every woman.

I particularly enjoy the way she ends each chapter with a thoughtful, fun exercise for readers to enrich their own lives in a meaningful way. Mary Fran's 'dirty words' truly are the words that make up a woman's life in the real world. This latest book from Mary Fran is a must-read for an entertaining break while also offering insights we can all appreciate and incorporate into our lives. And we all benefit from laughing more!"

~**Brenda Krueger Huffman, Founder & CEO, Women's Voices Media, LLC, Publisher**—*Women's Voices Magazine*, www.womensvoicesmagazine.com

"Mary Fran Bontempo nails it in *The Woman's Book of Dirty Words*. Bontempo's knack for presenting the modern woman's life experience is not only hilarious, but insightful and honest. By showing women how we can redefine words that have become 'dirty' to us, Bontempo ultimately teaches us that we can redefine our lives and recapture our sense of fun."

> ~Selena Rezvani, *ForbesWoman.com* columnist and author of *Pushback: How Smart Women Ask and Stand Up For What They Want*, www.selenarezvani.com

"Bravo! Mary Fran Bontempo cleverly gives women valuable advice while making us laugh at ourselves. She brilliantly captures the things we all do that make us (and our loved ones!) crazy, then addresses them with her trademark humor and insight. As a wife and mother, a television talk show host, and an aging baby boomer, I related to each and every word and found myself nodding along and smiling at each chapter. It's a MUST READ for women of all ages!"

> ~Lynn Doyle, 10 time Emmy-winning talk show host/president LDTV, LLC television production, www.lynndoyle.net

"Mary Fran has done it again. The insightful, fun, and funny Mom-of-All-Trades has extended the *Not Ready for Granny Panties* journey in *The Woman's Book of Dirty Words*. She simultaneously shares with us more funny, relatable stories, and extends them into usable tips. 'VACATION,' my personal favorite, takes Mary Fran's tip to 'do one thing that scares you every day' as she advises in *Not Ready for Granny Panties* and makes it applicable to today's modern mom out on the road, because as every woman knows, a family vacation can be one scary ordeal! Read this book. Gift this book. You are sure to enjoy this book."

> **~Jill L. Hickey, Founder, Radio Talk Show Host & Blogger—*The Not So Soccer Mom*, www.thenotsosoccermom.com. Owner, Express Pros Staffing, KC North**

"This book will make you laugh, think, and will stir emotions and memories of your past. Mary Fran's insights, humor, and storytelling will have you realize that you are in the company of so many other women when cringing as you hear these dirty words. A great read to lighten your heart, laugh, and understand the true meaning behind these everyday words that can strike fear into the hearts of women."

> **~Sara Canuso, President, Women That Influence, www.womenthatinfluence.com**

"Laughter—a noun. Laugh—a verb. Both connote the feelings of joy and light-heartedness that Mary Fran Bontempo's book, *The Woman's Book of Dirty Words,* elicits so well. Fun and accurate, every chapter made me laugh out loud. From the words 'vacation' and 'holiday' to 'relax' and 'balance,' she gets what it means to be a 21st century working woman trying to age gracefully while balancing the demands of family, work, friends, and life; trying to find ways to relax during vacation (LOL); and knowing that every 'holiday,' means more work than play. She approaches the topic with humor and insight. Her *Not Ready for Granny Panties* books are a must-read for men and women alike!"

~Gina F. Rubel, President and CEO, Furia Rubel Communications, Inc., www.furiarubel.com

"Mary Fran Bontempo has written yet another over-the-moon-and-back humorous book that is relatable beyond measure. I highly recommend *The Woman's Book of Dirty Words* to not only women, but to the men who love them, as they'll receive a double dose of reality and what certain words mean to us. Truly an enjoyable, delightful and important book. Mary Fran communicates what we feel!"

~Nancy Ferrari, Radio/TV Personality, Success Coach, www.nancyferrari.com

"Mary Fran has done it again! She has found a wonderful way with humor and grace to help us laugh at ourselves and at the same time, learn how to live life to the fullest. I found myself laughing and reflecting simultaneously as she took familiar words such as vacation and dinner, to help create a new sense of awareness about how our words truly impact our lives. Mary Fran is a genius when it comes to looking at what might be taboos or uncomfortable situations, and talking about them with wisdom and humor. She really gets us thinking about the everyday words in our lives and all the special experiences (and may be not so special experiences) inherent in a routine day. Mary Fran's book *The Woman's Book of Dirty Words* is not only funny but gives the reader a chance to look at life's complexities and challenges, while still finding the true joy of living life each day to its fullest. A must-read for all woman who use these 'dirty' words every day!"

~**Lynnis Woods-Mullins, Wellness Expert for Women Over 40, Publisher—***Wellness Woman 40 and Beyond* **E-Magazine, www.praiseworks.biz**

"Mary Fran Bontempo has done it again! Her latest book provides a glimpse into the grind of womanhood while offering simple, clear solutions to the emotional stressors we face in our day to day lives. Her easy wit and supportive style engender the feeling of sitting down to share a cup of tea with a close girlfriend. As a psychotherapist, I will recommend this book to my female patients who struggle with everyday stressors. Thanks for giving us permission to be something other than 'Nice,' Mary Fran Bontempo!"

> **~Ellen J. Faulkner, Ph.D., N.C.PsyA., www.faulknertherapy.net**

"Mary Fran Bontempo's new book, *The Woman's Book of Dirty Words*, is a true testament to the fact that we women share an intimate connection—and aversion—to our 'dirty words.' Mary Fran's ability to see the humor in all things related to those words that make us cringe allows readers to enjoy a wonderful ride of familiar scenarios, while laughing through it all. That type of connection is one of Mary Fran's best qualities. She encourages her readers to tweak their lives to bring back their own joy. It was a sincere pleasure to interview her, and learn some life lessons as well!"

> **~Susan Rocco, Founder & Host of Women to Watch, www.women2watch.net**

"I've followed Mary Fran over the years and she is one of the funniest women I've ever met. This summer she shared with me that she really was not ready for those granny panties but she was going to be a grandma! Fast forward to her new book, and though she may be wearing figurative granny panties, her 'dirty words' are relatable for women of all ages. As with her previous books, I laughed out loud. Mary Fran proves grannies can still have style!"

~**Joey Fortman, Founder—Real Mom Media, LLC, www.RealMomMedia.com**

"Awesome read! Mary Fran has an amazing writing style that left me laughing out loud, but also thinking seriously about the ways in which women maneuver around these 'dirty words.' When an author can make me feel like she is speaking directly to my experiences, it creates a feeling of support within. This book will be invaluable for any woman who is ready to claim her power."

~**Lee Anne Englert, LPC, Holistic Therapist, www.leeanneenglert.com**

"I haven't laughed this hard in a while. Every woman who knows those dirty words and all that's behind them should read this book to lighten the moment. Mary Fran's descriptions resonate with me because her story is born of an awareness that through all those crappy experiences, there's only so much you can do. She brings levity to my seriousness and who doesn't need to learn how to laugh at themselves more? Thank you, Mary Fran!"

> ~Denice Whiteley, Founder, Denice Whiteley Virtual Assistance, www.denicewhiteley.com

"Not only does Mary Fran really teach women how to stop, look at ourselves in the mirror, and really examine who and what we are in our lives, she has a fun and energizing way of making you feel good about yourself while showing you how to improve your life. She is a wife, a mom, and a great person who really wants you to learn about taking care of the busy, crazy, loving, thoughtful female!! I look so forward to hearing her present and reading her books. Her latest is a fun read that helps put into perspective what truly is important in life. Enjoy every word!"

> ~Marcia Zaruba O'Connor, CEO, The O'Connor Group, www.tocgrp.com

"Connected. This is how I felt when reading Mary Fran's book. As I read, I kept asking myself 'how does she know me so well?' She writes about the common threads of insanity of our lives as women and then gives us permission to let go. I instantly connected to the common crazy themes that bond us women, and even more connected to myself for realizing 'someone gets me.' From my crazy inner self making lists, doing laundry on vacation, and buying three sets of paper plates for a baby shower, I felt as if Mary Fran was speaking directly to me. She is as authentic as she is inspiring.

With each chapter I was guided through an understanding, given outstanding advice, told to get over my insanity, and encouraged to examine how to improve. As I read it was as if she had somehow interviewed me and the way that I think about the world. Mary Fran is a rare find as an author."

>~Jennifer L. Gardella, PhD, Your Social Media Expert, Founder, Your Social Media Hour, www.jennifergardella.com

"In a most comical manner, using a unique line-up of 'dirty' words, the author lightly treads on women's ridiculous lists of self-limitations. Nice? Relax? Balance? Ha! They all sound so innocent. Yet for us female caretakers, innocence takes on a frenetic quality as we perfectly 'should' ourselves to death. Bontempo's self-deprecating and witty writing style makes for a quick, yet thought-provoking read that may make us rethink our prior reaction to today's 'dirty word.'"

> ~Chrysa Smith, Author, *The Adventures of the Poodle Posse*—Mom's Choice Silver Medal winner, Dove Foundation endorsement, www.wellbredbook.net

"The *Woman's Book of Dirty Words* is a lighthearted but no-nonsense book that sheds light on the current reality of every day demands and pressures on women. The author's insights and invitation to put oneself first will help women reclaim and enjoy their lives. I absolutely loved this fun, quick read and highly recommend Mary Fran Bontempo as an author and a speaker."

> ~Jamie Broderick, Founder and CEO— Network Now Connections LLC, www.networknowconnections.com

"Who would have anticipated a visceral reaction to words like 'vacation,' 'holiday' and 'dinner'? I squirmed; I bit my lip. More important, I laughed. Once again Mary Fran has, in her crosshairs, the heavy baggage we women carry. And once again, she's helping us turn those suitcases into fanny packs. So now I can truly relax...which is now, thanks to Mary Fran, no longer a dirty word."

~Carla Merolla Odell, Founder, "Tell It Like It Was," www.carlamerollaodell.com

The Woman's Book of Dirty Words

A *Not Ready for Granny Panties* Book

By: Mary Fran Bontempo

With Illustrations by
Pat Achilles

About *Not Ready For Granny Panties*—The Blog

Several years ago, I found myself surfing the Internet in search of a place where I could find content geared toward me—a middle-aged woman who didn't feel, or particularly want to act, middle-aged. I was looking for fun stuff, interesting stuff that wasn't trying to "inspire" me, jam a message down my throat, or remind me of the endless array of physical ailments that came with aging and offer "solutions."

In fact, I wanted to avoid the term "aging" at all costs. If I needed to be reminded that I was no longer 20, all I had to do was look in a mirror. Reading about it ad nauseam on the Internet was not on my "to do" list.

I also was looking for a site that wouldn't give me a migraine with a thousand links to click, fourteen drop-down menu items per page heading and a dizzying array of things that flashed, beeped, or talked to me without any initiation on my part. (Just try to find the stop button on those videos that start automatically.)

You know what? The pickins' were mighty slim. So I decided to start my own site, a place where women like me could go and have a few minutes of fun every day. A place where I could talk about things that made me laugh, as well as movies, food, fashion, and anything else that just made me feel good.

That's how the blog, **Not Ready for Granny Panties,** was born. Along with the help of some really smart, wonderful women (Pat Achilles, Chrysa Smith, and Carmen Ferreiro-Esteban), I developed a site just for us—and for you, www.notreadyforgrannypanties.com.

Girls just wanna have fun, and we *NRFGP* gals realized, through sharing with readers, that none of us was ready to put on the big bloomers and consign ourselves to Granny Panties, either literal or figurative. As we brought our take on life to *NRFGP*, we realized that there was more to say, about life in the middle and how we can live it to the fullest as the fabulous, glorious creatures we are.

This book is book two of that "more to say." I'm certain other things will follow, as I've never been known to let anything go gently. But I also think that at this point, gentle isn't going to get me, or you, where I want to go, which is as far away as possible from a pair of Granny Panties.

So after you've finished the book, remember to stick with us and check out the *NRFGP* blog at www.notreadyforgrannypanties.com every day for a daily dose of fun and celebration of life in the middle with "girls" just like you! And visit me at www.maryfranbontempo.com. I'd love to hear from you!

For Dave,

David, Laura, Megan, Kelly, Emma & Jimmy,

who inspire me every day

Table of Contents

Introduction		1
Chapter 1:	What's in a Word?	5
Chapter 2:	Vacation	11
Chapter 3:	Dinner	25
Chapter 4:	Nice	37
Chapter 5:	No	49
Chapter 6:	Relax	61
Chapter 7:	Holidays	73
Chapter 8:	Comfortable	87
Chapter 9:	Fine	101
Chapter 10:	Change	113
Chapter 11:	Balance	125
Chapter 12:	Adventure	137
Chapter 13:	Epilogue	147

Introduction

I'm the *Not Ready for Granny Panties* lady. At least that's how I've been described on more than one occasion. In fact, it's how I've sometimes described myself.

Which is okay, because it's true. Several years ago, after witnessing the demise of the newspapers for which I was writing and falling into an epic funk, I decided to start the blog, *Not Ready for Granny Panties*, because, well, I wasn't. Ready for granny panties, that is.

Chronologically, I most certainly was ready for granny panties, given that all of my kids were in their twenties and more than able to procreate. (They didn't, which back then was a good thing, but another story entirely.)

My aversion to granny panties had far less to do with my fears of being old enough to be a grandmother and far more to do with what I perceived as my gradual slide into irrelevance, oblivion, and boredom as I passed the half-century mark. (Yeesh, that still sounds awful.)

The sidelining of women over a certain age is nothing new. The pursuit of youth in our culture almost makes aging a sin, unless you're a guy and happen to look like George Clooney, in which case you're still astoundingly gorgeous and able to snag a spouse almost twenty years your junior. (Damn him. And her, too, now that I think of it.)

The dearth of great movie and television roles for older women is routinely bemoaned by the Hollywood glitterati, which is a shame for them, but even worse for those of us who never did and never will have a shot at that kind of platform to actually bemoan anything. We're expected to do what will make everyone around us comfortable and quietly fade into the background.

Well, um, no. Being quiet about anything has never been my strong suit, but when everything in my life started to go to hell around a decade ago, I got very quiet, because I didn't know what else to do.

That approach got me exactly nowhere, so I decided to start speaking up, on behalf of myself and on behalf of other women, both older and not so old. I wasn't sure if what I had to say would resonate, but it felt pretty good to write about my "stuff" and get things off my chest, and it was a lot cheaper than therapy.

It turned out that what I felt, and subsequently said, rang a lot more bells than I could have imagined.

We women, regardless of where we are in life, all pretty much want the same things: love, peace, health, and security (lots of money doesn't hurt, either)—for ourselves and our families. The details of our lives might be different, but the larger stories are basically the same.

What I found, though, was that even though we all wanted the same things, when it came to getting them, we were often our own worst enemies. And a lot of it had to do with our self-talk, which often means getting ourselves out of granny panties —not the literal ones, the ones we wear in our heads that keep us from believing we can and should have what we want in life.

So through the *Not Ready for Granny Panties* platforms (blog, books, and other, variously placed musings), I've made it my business to reach out to women—all types and ages of women—to find out how we think and how we can tweak our inner lives to make our outer lives better. And I try to do it with laughter, because most days, you're a hair's breadth away from laughing or crying, so you might as well laugh.

Finally, I am a grandmother now, and it's not half as bad as I feared. In fact, it's pretty great, which just goes to prove that the reality of a situation might not be something to fear, but rather the exact opposite.

So here's to getting rid of your mental granny panties, no matter your age, and talking yourself into living a wonderful life!

Chapter 1

What's in a Word?

We women like to talk.

We talk to the tune of around 20,000 words per day, if current science is to be believed. We talk to commune with our girlfriends, sisters and mothers, we talk to issue directives to our kids and families, we talk to share our feelings (ad nauseum, if you ask our husbands and partners), we talk at work, we talk at play, sometimes we even talk in our sleep.

Words are kind of our thing. We should be word experts. So why is it that certain words send us over the edge?

Why is it, that when lobbed in our direction in conversation, or sometimes even merely thought about, certain words make us crazy? Crazier, that is. Let's be honest, we gals are all a little off center to begin with.

Words are powerful instruments. Uniquely the province of humans, we rely on words to fuel most of our communication with the world (although the influence of a well-placed eye roll is not to be underestimated).

Generally, a word conveys a specific idea, an idea that is readily understood by those sharing the language of the word. A dog is a four-legged domesticated animal that most often exists as a pet for humans. Easy enough.

Yet, over time, even the simplest, most obvious word can take on new meaning, as when a dog serves to describe the jerk of a guy who just broke your daughter's heart. There are other words to describe him as well, but let's stick to those acceptable in polite conversation.

Many words in the English language have multiple meanings, either by definition or connotation. Look at the word "run" in the following sentences:

Run and get the flashlight.
Tom is going to **run** for class president.
The Phillies scored a home **run**.
Don't **run** to your mother with every little complaint, you're supposed to be a grown-up, what's wrong with you?

Okay, that last one was a run-on. And a little hysterical. Sorry.

But you get the idea. Words can have multiple meanings, all of which are acceptable and recognizable to the general populace. The general populace not operating with the mind of a stressed-out, overwhelmed, time-challenged, can't-do-everything-myself woman, that is.

To us, any number of words, despite appearing innocent to men, children, and even some women as yet inexperienced in the ways of familial bliss (read: single women whose crazy is unrelated to raising a family), can create profound anxiety, angst, worry, frustration, and even fear.

These words are not complex, and quite often, the aforementioned men, children, and single women react to them with eager anticipation and, dare I say, pleasure. But for other women, particularly mothers, it's a different story. For us, these words make comedian George Carlin's list of "Seven Words You Can Never Say on Television" read like a nursery rhyme.

Because of our position in the hierarchy of family life, which translates into the person in charge of everybody's everything, certain words come equipped with a negative charge that's hard for us to counteract. We hear them, and while everyone in the family around us may be smiling and dancing with anticipation at the future joy the word is sure to bring to one and all, we're gritting our teeth in dread.

We know the reality behind some words is not that simple.

However, there is some good news. Most of the dread we attach to words that everyone else likes is, to some degree, of our own making. As such, we can fix it. Well, maybe not fix it entirely, but at least quell the urge to run screaming into the street whenever a certain word crops up in conversation. Sometimes, that's got to be enough.

So let's take a look at some "Dirty Words." Those words that should make us happy but too often induce a panic attack. With any luck, the next time you hear one, you'll smile instead of bursting into tears.

Chapter 2

Vacation

Va·ca·tion

noun

1. a period of time when work, study, or other regular activity is suspended
2. time spent away from home in pursuit of travel, recreation, or rest
3. freedom from regular obligations, business, or school

Was there ever a word that got your eight-year-old juices flowing like the word vacation?

To your eight-year-old self, vacation was the lottery-winning jackpot of words. It either signaled the end of school and three months of goofing off, or holidays like Christmas and Thanksgiving, which also equaled presents—a double bonus.

It meant, as noted in the definition above, FREEDOM. Freedom from doing all of the stuff a kid hates to do, which at eight primarily involves anything connected with school. No more pencils, no more books, no more teachers' dirty looks—

mainly because the people giving us dirty looks on vacation were our mothers.

For my childhood self, vacation also meant the beach, or rather, the one week each year when my family travelled for our vacation to the Jersey shore. During approximately eighty-six trips from house to car, we would stuff our station wagon to the bursting point with clothes for six people, sheets, towels, sun tan lotion (sunscreen wasn't even on the radar back then), beach chairs, a beach umbrella, toys, and of course, food. After the house rental was paid, there was usually enough left for one full meal out, with some treats sprinkled through the week. But the rest of the time, my mother cooked.

Once the car was packed, we'd pile in, my youngest brother relegated to the fold up seat far in the rear of the station wagon. (I'm pretty sure those seats are now illegal.) At least I think he was back there. There was so much stuff in the car, no one could see or hear him for the entire trip. But he's in the pictures and I kind of remember him hanging around, so I guess he was along for the ride.

When we arrived at our destination, after a three-hour odyssey on the Atlantic City Expressway during which it was a crap shoot as to whether or not we'd join the parade of overheated vehicles on the side of the road, the unloading commenced, necessitating another eighty-six trips into the rental house. At least every three minutes during this process, one of the four kids would plaintively ask, "Can we go to the beach after this?" at which point my mother or father would bark, "Can we just get this done first?" while handing the offender another bag or suitcase to carry inside.

Three hours later, when we did finally make our way to the beach, it was hard to tell that we left anything back at the house, so loaded down were we with the requisite beach gear. That is, my parents were loaded down. We kids were allowed to grab a sand bucket and run towards the water to escape the blistering sand, a calculated move by my parents: Make the kids carry stuff and listen to them cry when their feet burn or carry all the crap ourselves and have at least a few minutes peace? They let us run.

At week's end, sunburned and happily exhausted, we reversed the entire process and made our way back to Philadelphia, the snarled traffic, oppressive heat and invisible little brother once again our travel companions.

Oh, how I loved those vacations. I could never quite understand why my parents didn't.

Truth be told, my father enjoyed himself a little more than my mom. Once he delivered us safely to the destination and excepting the daily trudges to the beach and dips into his wallet, he was able to be off duty, at least for a while. (I'm sure the Jack Daniels helped significantly.)

My mother had no such respite. Mothers rarely do. My mother was still charged with feeding, clothing, washing, and overseeing four children in a "home" that wasn't her own. Four children who, despite the fact that they were on vacation, were, by turns, tired, cranky, sunburned, hot, thirsty, and overwhelmed by "fun."

I recall one summer when my mother was washing a glass, which broke and cut her hand. She had to go to the emergency room for stitches and was gone for hours. I, always neurotic, was certain she wasn't coming back. Looking through my own "mom glasses" now, I imagine those few hours of peace and quiet in the E.R. were the highlight of her trip that year.

So you have you as your eight-year-old self on vacation. The beach, the boardwalk, the carefree days, the forbidden foods suddenly allowed and indulged in, the late bed times, the fun, fun, fun!

Now fast forward twenty or thirty years, to the you who is dragging kids on your family's own annual vacation. Who do you see now? If you're anything like me, you see your mother. With your face. That's right; now, when you go on vacation, you are your mother, which, all by itself, is enough to send any woman over the edge. Add in several tired, cranky kids, a sub-par hotel or beach rental and seventeen suitcases, coolers, and bags full of clothes, food, toys, sheets, towels, medicine, flip-flops, beach chairs, etc., etc., etc., and, well...

Is it any wonder "vacation" is a dirty word for women?

It should get better as we, and our families, get older. After all, teens can carry more than a bucket and shovel to the beach. However, they can also carry surly teenaged attitudes about family vacations, frequently turning the entire adventure into a grumble fest about how they're "too old for this stuff" and pushing everyone's patience to the limit, while whining about how their friends got to go to Disney World or Aruba together for their vacation. Yeah, sign me up.

If you manage to get the family together once the kids have hit the college years and beyond, you're then often presented with the issue of the "significant other," who must be included in every family event, despite the permanence, or lack of permanence, of the relationship in your child's life. Deny access and risk your own kid refusing to take part. Allow it and be forced to deal with the "Where is everyone sleeping?" question. What parent doesn't want to think of their kid sleeping with a significant other on vacation, and on the sheets you provided? I mean, let's add that image to the mental photo album. Or let's not.

And you are still the one bringing the sheets, towels, food, toilet paper, paper towels, toothpaste, and other household supplies—you know, the stuff everyone thinks magically appears in the cabinets at home—but now you're loading it into the car yourself, because the children you once forced to act as manual labor have jobs, or school, or other commitments, ones that don't include loading—or unloading—the car.

Further, as the instigator, or perpetrator of the family vacation (and at times, it does feel like you're perpetrating a crime, let's face it), you're also usually responsible for the bulk of the trip financially, even if the kids are older. As such, use the rule of thumb for home repairs—whatever you figure it's gonna cost, double it.

Notice we haven't even touched on vacations involving airplanes, airports, countless security checks and body searches, hotels, lost reservations and luggage, passports, the movie *Taken*, and kids who insist they can find their way around a foreign country even though they can't find the hamper in their rooms at home.

Sounds like decades and decades of fun, doesn't it? Oh yes, vacation is not only a dirty word for women, sometimes it's downright filthy.

So, what's the solution, aside from emptying the vacation bank account and buying a one-way ticket to a really expensive spa in California?

First, and most important, LOWER YOUR EXPECTATIONS.

The annual vacation is the Holy Grail of family experiences. We look to the vacation to create memories meant to last a lifetime, to be recounted lovingly through the years as an example of how wonderful our togetherness was.

Except that it often isn't. The perfect family vacation simply doesn't exist, and the expectations we hold for it all but guarantee its failure. Think Chevy Chase and the trip to Wally World in *National Lampoon's Vacation*. Dead old lady strapped to the roof, anyone? Family vacations may have their wonderful moments, but if you're expecting perfection, what you're more likely to get is a big suitcase full of disappointment.

So relax, already. I mean, isn't that the point of a vacation anyway?

The most you should expect from a family vacation is the opportunity to spend some time together doing something different, somewhere different. And notice I didn't even say "quality" time. Because everyone's definition of that is different, and forcing your definition on everyone else is a recipe for disaster.

Time together, doing something different from the normal routine has all the potential necessary to become something else. Something better than the norm, especially if the experience is allowed to evolve into whatever it's going to be. Remember that most of the memories we hold dear come from experiences that just happened. They are rarely entire events, but rather moments that came from within events or places and grew organically.

Which brings us to point number two: Leave the laminated and itemized vacation planner at home. We women lose our minds over vacation planning, whether it's about travel arrangements, sleeping arrangements, packing, food, itineraries, etc., etc. Some of it's necessary. I mean, if you don't want to sleep in your car or a bus station, you have to book a hotel, but much of our incessant planning isn't. Much of it is about our demented need to control everybody's everything, including dictating every moment of the one thing we're all supposed to be doing to get away from our tightly wound lives—a restful, relaxing vacation. (And yes, I was the one with the pages-long lists in Disney World, dictating everything from when we would get to the parks, to where we would eat, to which lines we should stand in for the rides. I think my family hated me and now, I kind of hate myself.)

Instead, have a few "musts"—with the option of ditching should you change your mind—and go with the flow. If you're flying everyone to Disney World, of course you need to plan, but don't OVER-plan. Make reservations for special meals once or twice, and then wing it. Decide which park you're going to visit, choose a few must-see attractions, and then give everyone the option of trying other things or heading back to the pool for an afternoon of splashing and lounging.

If you're beach-bound for a vacation, plan for plenty of time sitting on the sand, and not much else. Beaches offer their own built-in options; planning by obsessive women is unnecessary. Apply the same guidelines for meals—one or two special outings—and then just let whatever happens, happen. A week of pizza and ice cream isn't going to kill anyone.

Further, make sure you allow everyone an activity of their choice, in which everyone participates or they can indulge in themselves, if they're old enough. Giving everyone the option to choose an activity of their own can head off a mutiny when you present your "have to" vacation musts, as in, "Yes, you *have to* do this with us."

It's not a bad idea to work in some exercise time for yourself either, if you're so inclined. Running away, as long as you return, will clear your head, not to mention provide an outlet for the adrenaline build-up that will occasionally threaten to derail your vacation nirvana. And when you stop running, don't forget to whip out that trashy novel you hid in your bag, or the *People Magazine* you picked up at the convenience store. After all, what's a great vacation without mindless drivel filling your head?

Speaking of heads, don't forget headphones, which will attach to iPods, tablets or other electronic devices. Although your instinct may be to ban these entirely, they can be just the antidote to too much togetherness, the scorpion sting of many family vacations. Provided no one is glued to their devices the entire time, when you all just can't stand to look at one another for one more minute, allow, no DEMAND, that everyone plug in and tune out for a while. It could be your salvation.

As could a little independence, especially before the vacation, in the form of everyone packing for themselves. Now before you dissolve into hysterical laughter, with images of no one bringing any underwear, know that making everyone responsible for their own packing is possible. And it's all in the list.

Every woman is a list-maker. From grocery lists, "to-do" lists, appointment lists, and so on, we're expert list-makers. So do what you do best. Make a list of what everyone should bring (DON'T OVER-PACK!), distribute said lists, have everyone lay out their clothing on their beds, inspect to see they've got what they need and stick it all in a suitcase. Voila. Your kids have autonomy over their wardrobe and you don't have to pack for everyone. (Just make sure you stop this practice before the kids graduate from high school. It's embarrassing when your 22-year-old son tells you he's not packed for the next day's trip because you never gave him his packing list.)

If someone forgets something, buy it or do without. Unless you're going to the Amazon Jungle, it's a safe bet you'll find a store that has t-shirts.

While we're on the subject of clothing, one more suggestion, which may go against every fiber of your being. Do the laundry while you're away.

Think about it. Is there anything that destroys the vacation Zen faster than a laundry room full of dirty clothes when you get home? If at all possible, the day before you leave, throw in at least a few loads of laundry, maybe while you're relaxing by the pool. Then, when you get back to reality, and your house, everyone puts away clean clothes and you aren't digging out from under a mountain of sandy, smelly shorts for a week.

Minimalism, in terms of expectations, packing, meals, and yes, even togetherness—though that's supposed to be the point of a family vacation—can be the saving grace of the entire experience. Don't expect too much, don't plan much, don't pack much, don't eat too much, and get the heck away from each other once in a while.

It's the recipe for a perfect vacation.

Try This!

Think about your last vacation. Write down three things that caused problems, tensions or arguments. Next to each item, write how the problem could have been solved, or better yet, avoided.

1._____

_____

2._____

_____

3._____

_____

Next, write down three things that went well, helping to make wonderful vacation memories. Next to each, write how you could create similar moments on future vacations.

1._____

_____

2._____

_____

3._____

_____

Finally, write down five things you would personally like to do on your next vacation. When your vacation comes around, DO THEM!

1._____

2._____

3._____

4._____

5._____

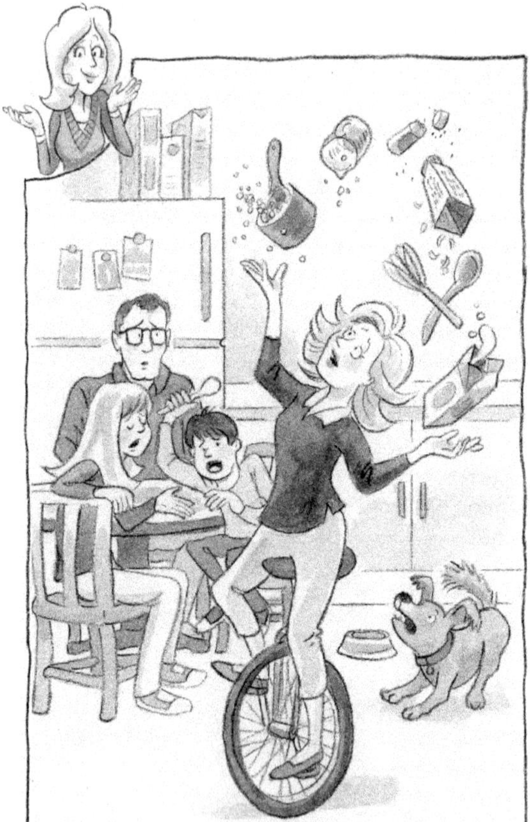

# Chapter 3

Dinner

Din·ner

noun

1. the main meal of a day, usually eaten in the evening
2. a formal meal marking a special occasion or in honor of a particular person

Well, this hardly seems like a big deal, now does it?

I mean, it's a meal, occasionally a formal one, usually eaten in the evening. Why would a word like dinner get a gal's knickers in a knot?

I'll tell you why.

Do you remember that Norman Rockwell picture of Thanksgiving Dinner, where multiple generations of smiling family members gather around a table set with china and crystal on a pristine white table cloth as the family matriarch lovingly offers a perfectly browned turkey to her adoring relatives?

My dinners don't look anything like that.

First off, my dinners don't start at dinner time. They usually start around mid-morning, when the question, "What am I going to make for dinner?" makes its first appearance of the day. It's impossible to answer the question at that time, as I'm usually not at home and have zero recall of what's in the freezer or pantry aside from some chicken with a healthy case of freezer-burn and a half-filled box of pasta.

So I shelve the question until mid-afternoon, no more equipped to answer it as I'm still not home, but I resolve to "pick something up for dinner" while making my rounds to the bank, the dry cleaners, and the drug store. When I get home, I realize I never did get around to the grocery store, at which point I try to figure out exactly how to make freezer-burned chicken and a half-box of pasta even remotely palatable, let alone nutritious.

Sound familiar?

Making dinner is one of womanhood's most relentless jobs, especially if you're a mother, primarily because kids have an annoying habit of wanting to be fed every evening. Of course, they also want to eat in the morning and at lunch, too. But somehow those meals pale in comparison to the acrobatics involved in putting dinner on the table for a family every single night.

Bearing the responsibility for feeding and watering the masses three times a day, every day is exhausting. Yet a box of Cheerios and milk can take the pain out of breakfast, just as a PB&J can solve a lunch dilemma with enough time left over to grab an apple, a juice box, and some string cheese. Voila —a balanced, and only partially processed, offering.

Dinner is something else entirely. Dinner requires thought—the last thing a tired woman wants to do at 6:00 p.m. How many times have you stumbled in the door and thought, *What I wouldn't give to just pour myself a bowl of those Cheerios, grab a glass of wine, and call it a day.* (Who says wine doesn't go with Cheerios?)

But, noooooo! Not only do you have to figure out what to serve everyone, but you also have to recall everyone's likes and dislikes and cook accordingly. And you will never accommodate everyone's likes and dislikes. Rarely does dinner time pass in any home in the country without the requisite complaint, "Oh no, we're having that? I hate that! Do I have to eat it?"

When I was growing up, the answer was, "Yes" or starve. Of course, we would never have been allowed to starve, but we didn't know that. My dad was a scary guy. When he said, "Eat it," we ate it. My mother made it, it was on the plate, we ate it. Period.

But somewhere along the line, mothers decided that their kids had to be happy all of the time, and that included dinner. Studies (likely conducted by some disgruntled guy whose mother made him eat his broccoli) showed that forcing children to eat foods they didn't like could contribute to life-long eating problems. So we turned ourselves into short-order cooks and started whipping up multiple offerings at dinner. Suzy doesn't like meat, so she gets chicken, Billy won't eat rice, so it's mashed potatoes for him and just to be sure everyone gets a vegetable, it's corn, peas, broccoli and raw baby carrots. Oh, and don't forget the ranch dressing for dipping. The children must have their ranch dressing for dipping. Kids will eat a sweat sock if it's dipped in ranch dressing.

If you're wondering, this is the line of thinking that made me realize wine goes perfectly with Cheerios—and anything else a woman has the energy to eat herself after preparing fifteen different options at every meal.

It's an impossible model to maintain, especially since you'd have to have the contents of an entire grocery store constantly on hand to make a week's worth of meals. No one has enough food available to do that—see freezer-burned chicken and half a box of pasta, above. Which leads to the more common scenario of staring into the freezer at 6:00, dragging out the chicken (prepare yourself for the "Chicken again?!" outcry), boiling the pasta and hoping there's a jar of applesauce hidden behind those Cheerios.

Whining ensues, plates are left barely touched and women are served yet another heaping helping of guilt for not providing a nutritious meal at dinner.

It's all quite ironic, given America's fascination with cooking. We love cooking shows—*Top Chef, The Chew, Chopped, Hell's Kitchen*, and of course, the entire Food Network. We watch these shows ad nauseum, wanting nothing more than to replicate the delicious, nutritious, beautiful (yes, they're always beautiful) meals offered up with ease by chefs advising viewers to just "add a little pancetta," "sauté with fresh herbs," and "pop this into the oven for 20 minutes."

Simple, really, especially if you have a staff buying, chopping, and readying ingredients in an array of little bowls lined up in the order in which they're needed while someone off camera stands at the ready with the spatula you misplaced. Let's not forget the director, who edits out the spills, burns, messes, and blood when you accidentally cut your finger while rushing to get everything on the table before everyone flies out the door to after-dinner practices, games, and activities.

Of course, that's assuming they show up to eat in the first place.

On those rare occasions when you do manage to get your act together and come up with something substantial and palatable, dinner attendance is still a crap shoot. On any given night, you could prepare for five and have two, seven, three, or none show up at the table. You alternately forgo food yourself to stretch the meal and feed whomever your kids invited to stay without telling you ("Oh don't worry about me; I had a late lunch,") or pack everything away in containers that will end up buried in the back of the fridge, covered in mold, as God forbid that anyone eats leftovers.

Lest you think the pressure subsides as the kids grow older and leave home, allow me to disillusion you. First of all, they never leave home, and second, around 6:00 p.m. every evening, they still ask the same question, albeit couched in terms meant to imply that you'll be let off the hook should you answer in the negative: "Hey, Mom, are you cooking tonight?" Translation: "I'm still here, I'm still your kid and I'm still hungry. What's for dinner and no, you're not off the hook yet."

That is why the word, "dinner," can send a woman over the edge.

What to do, other than hire a full-time chef or resort to a fridge and pantry stocked with food loaded with so many preservatives that it never expires and also glows in the dark?

First and most important, LOWER THEIR EXPECTATIONS. This isn't a repeat of last chapter's advice, but it's close. Note that this time, the expectations you're lowering belong to other people, namely, those people in your home who expect you to make multiple dishes at every dinner to accommodate everyone's tastes.

If there were ever a time to revert to the way things "used to be," this is it. Dad, wherever you are, you were right. If a mom makes it and it ends up on the plate, that's what's for dinner. Period. Eat it or don't eat it. But if you don't eat it and you're under the age of eighteen, don't expect to wander into the kitchen after the meal is over and graze through junk to appease your appetite. When the plates are cleared, dinner is over, and the kitchen is closed until breakfast the next morning, unless you clean up your own mess after you're done grazing, which you won't do, so see: THE KITCHEN IS CLOSED, above.

It's okay to make some concessions to the multiple choice options, but make them easy concessions, such as offering both raw carrots and broccoli to ensure everyone has a vegetable option that requires next to no work from you. Otherwise, everyone eats what's set on the table, unless they're highly allergic, in which case I'm guessing you wouldn't be serving it anyway.

When everyone stops expecting to find a restaurant's worth of menu options on the dinner table, they'll learn to eat what's in front of them. Unless you're at an actual restaurant, one from column A and one from column B shouldn't be a choice anyway.

While you're at it, lower your own expectations as well. You aren't a short-order cook; you're a busy woman faced with the never-ending job of feeding and watering the troops. The military has people who do that too, but it's their only job. It's far from your only job.

So keep a few standard-issue items always at the ready—a full box or two of pasta along with a decent jarred sauce (I know, Nan, I'm committing a cardinal sin advocating jarred "gravy," but times have changed), ground turkey or beef for quick burgers, several pounds of chicken cutlets, boxed potatoes, a bag of stuffing, frozen vegetables, and a bag of baby carrots. And okay, the ranch dressing.

Obviously, the specific items aren't the point. The point is try to keep a few things always available that you know your family can choke down if you run out of options or time or both. On those nights when Old Mother Hubbard truly has nothing in her cupboard, and dinner consists of peanut butter and jelly crackers or the box of Bagel Bites you found in the back of the freezer, relax. Everyone will survive. In fact, your kids will likely see such meals as highlights on their dinner hit parade. With a glass of wine at the ready to wash it down, so will you.

Another trick—embrace the casserole, or the crock pot meal. When I was a kid, I hated casseroles, which, to me, translated as my mother took whatever she had in the fridge, tossed it in a bowl, added some kind of soup and baked it. Which is what she did.

And what you should do, too, if time and necessity warrants. Or dig out your crock pot and Google some recipes. I've found some decent ones and nothing beats having dinner handled early in the morning and ready in the evening.

As your kids get older, have them take turns making dinner once every other week. It will teach them what a pain in the ass the whole process is and make them appreciate your efforts even more. Better yet, make them come along to the grocery store to shop for the ingredients for their meal. After two such excursions, you'll never hear another whisper of complaint.

When they're older still, just don't cook—at least not every night. Let them figure it out for themselves while you feast on Cheerios and wine. Offer them the leftovers housed in those containers in the fridge and remind them about how many people are starving in the world. Most young adults have a pretty active social conscience, so maybe you can guilt them into eating the leftovers. It's worth a shot, especially for anyone who loathes throwing away food as much as I do.

And for god's sake, stop watching those damn cooking shows. No good can come of setting yourself up for that kind of failure. If you must indulge, do so with no intention of replicating anything you see. Never, ever watch while you're hungry. Better to sit through a rerun of *Full House* than watch a professional chef create a fabulous meal you have no hope of making, let alone eating. In fact, before you turn on the TV, grab a menu to your favorite pizza place and keep the number on speed dial in your phone. If you're tempted to cook after an episode of Rachael Ray, pick up the phone and order a large pie.

Finally, remember that it's not all about the food. Sure, a great meal at the end of the day is wonderful, but so is conversation with the people you love. Family dinners can be frantic affairs, so try for at least one great meal weekly—and great conversations more often. Sitting around a table and connecting with family is the important part here, regardless of whether you're serving steak, pizza, or cereal.

And if all else fails, there's always the McDonald's dollar menu.

Try This!

Write down the names of three of your easiest, most reliable dinner recipes. After each, write down the ingredients you need for each dish. (Hint: If you need more than four main ingredients for any recipe, CHOOSE ANOTHER DISH.) Then, check your pantry and make sure you have the ingredients on hand to make any of the dishes at any time.

1._____

_____

2._____

_____

3._____

_____

Next, if you cook dinner for others, ask each person to describe their favorite "desperation dinner"—the things you serve when you didn't go shopping—and buy the stuff you needed to make anything above. Things like bagels, cereal and frozen pizza are acceptable. List each desperation dinner item below. Make sure you have the items for at least two desperation dinners a week in your pantry.

_____

_____

_____

_____

_____

_____

Finally, buy wine. Then drink it.

NICE-VEMBER
S
M
T
W
T
F
S
WORK PROJ. DUE
SCHOOL TRIP
CAR POOL
BAKE SALE
HEATER CLEANING 8 AM
HAIR CUT?
MEETING 2 PM
MOM DR. APPT
PTA
CAR POOL
SNACK SOCCER TEAM
CHARITY WORK
JIM'S BIRTHDAY PARTY
VISIT AUNT DORIS
BALLET CLASS
SHOP
SHOP MORE
COLOR CODE

Chapter 4

Nice

Nice

adjective

1. pleasing or pleasant
2. agreeable
3. friendly, delightful or kind

Talk about a wolf in sheep's clothing.

Take a close look at the word, nice. How many letters are in that word? Four. Four little letters. A four letter word.

Yes, ladies, nice is a four letter word. And it deserves to be handled with all the caution accorded to the other four letter words in your vocabulary.

Now, let me establish that I have nothing against four letter words. In fact, I find them rather useful for venting and letting off steam. I'm not advocating peppering your speech with them; using them to excess seems just plain lazy and obnoxious, but they do serve a purpose. They may be ugly, but used sparingly, they can have a paradoxically healing effect. And sometimes, as when you've lost your keys, you're stuck in traffic and late for a meeting, or the cable has gone out—again—nothing else will do.

Nice works differently. Nice is a liar, pretending to be, well, nice. It's a hijacker, intent on taking over your life. Nice masquerades as a benign, pleasant word (see, you can't even talk about it without sounding "nice") but is secretly infused with enough destructive properties to annihilate any woman.

There is another definition missing from the above that sticks to any woman labelled as nice faster and tighter than a soaking with Super Glue: doormat. Also, exhausted, frustrated, abused and martyr. Throw in submissive, bland, boring, neglected, and moments away from a breakdown. Yeah, that about covers it.

Nice is the queen of passive aggressive words. From the outset, little girls are taught to be nice. When we're nice, people smile at us, sometimes actually applaud us, which makes us happy. So we continue to aspire to nice, eventually becoming slaves to it, martyring ourselves to it, acting "nice" even when we feel anything but.

When we're being "nice," we do things we're "supposed to," things society dictates that nice girls would do. Maybe it starts when we're told to share our candy with our siblings because it's nice to share. Then we're offering to stay in and help a friend study for a test when we had tickets to a concert.

Next, we're picking up extra shifts at work to help out a co-worker even though we're over-worked and tired ourselves. Then, we're agreeing to head the fundraising committee at the kids' school, despite the fact that we have a major project due at work, our in-laws are coming to visit for a week, and the house is a mess.

But of course, we wouldn't want anyone to think we aren't nice, so, pile it on! However, after we're through being nice, we're cranky, miserable, exhausted, and thinking evil thoughts. Not very nice at all.

Nice is anything but benign. It's a loaded word that serves to trap any woman who falls for the lie that it's a character trait. Nice is quicksand. Do you remember those old movies where some schlub is running through the jungle or desert or some God-forsaken place and he ends up stumbling into quicksand? The more the poor trapped soul struggles to get free, the deeper he sinks, until there's nothing left but his hand sticking out of the muck, wriggling, until it, and he, disappears completely.

So it is with nice. Nice women are the ones who do absolutely everything—for everyone but themselves. Trying to be unfailingly nice, to meet the unattainable expectations she'll inevitably set in place for herself, will swallow a woman whole. Eventually, she will become the very antithesis of nice, instead turning into a simmering cauldron of resentment and anxiety. When a woman dedicates herself to being nice at all costs, she, too, will eventually disappear, much like the guy trapped in quicksand, losing her personality, her independence, and her very self to an impossible idol.

Have you ever noticed it's the "nice" women who are always asked to head the bake sale committee, volunteer for the charity drive, be the team mom, organize the office parties, pick up a carload of kids from the dance, host the holiday dinners, and on and on and on?

Take a look at that list. Is there anything on there that you'd really, really love to do? Any of those items that would have you wake up in the morning, jump out of bed and say, "Wow! I can't WAIT to (fill in the blank) today? (Some uninitiated souls might say they'd love to host a holiday dinner, but that's only because they've never hosted a holiday dinner. For more, see "Dinner," Chapter 3.) I'll answer for you: NO. No, no, and again, no.

The jobs nice women are asked to do are lousy jobs. The reason they are asked to do these lousy jobs is precisely because they are nice and people know they won't say, "No." Should you be known as a nice woman and say, "No" to a lousy job that someone assumes you'll take on with a smile, people will wonder what's wrong with you. Should you say, "No" more than once, people will brand you a "bitch" and talk about you behind your back.

Let them.

"Bitch" is one of those words that women fear. As much as we want the world to apply the "nice" label to us, we want to avoid the "bitch" label at all costs. No one wants to be labeled a bitch, especially if the name is bestowed by another woman, which makes it particularly hurtful. Bitches are mean and nasty—the women no one likes; at least that's what we're supposed to believe.

But in reality, genuine bitches are fascinating. They're powerful and they're ruthless. And if we admit it to ourselves, we can't take our eyes off them. We might even envy them a little, because the fact is, bitches get sh*t done.

Several years ago, Tina Fey did a riff on bitches on a *Saturday Night Live* segment. At the time, Fey was commenting on Hillary Clinton's 2008 presidential run for the nomination against Barack Obama, noting the some people were reluctant to get on board with Clinton because she'd been labeled a "bitch."

"Let me say something about that," Fey said. "She is. And so am I. Bitches get stuff done. That's why Catholic schools use nuns as teachers instead of priests. By the end of the year, you hated that bitch, but you knew the capital of Vermont."

The truth is every woman has a little bitch in her. And we need it. Because, like it or not, unless you're willing to occasionally put on your bitchy-girl panties, you're gonna get walked on.

Case in point: One day when my daughter, Laura, was living in Florida while completing a graduate program, she texted me after failing to pick up on a Face Time call that I initiated. (And let me say, thank God for Face Time. It allowed me to see my daughter and have breakfast with her almost daily via our phones and kept us both from crying all the time.)

Laura texted that she couldn't Face Time, because her cable was out and her Internet, needed for the call, was down. Further, Face Time wasn't her only problem. She needed to work on a huge school project that day and she needed the Internet to do it.

Laura had called the cable company and was informed, after 40 minutes of phone time and unsuccessful attempts at "unplug this, wait 30 seconds, plug in that, yadda, yadda, yadda," that they could probably get a service technician out a few days later.

At which point she put on her bitchy-girl pants.

"Listen," Laura said, "that is completely unacceptable. I pay you $120 a month for this service. I have a paper I need to submit to school by noon. You need to get someone out here within the next hour and get this fixed. And if you can't help me, then put a supervisor on the phone."

My daughter relayed all of this to me via the Face Time call that took place 20 minutes after I originally tried to reach her. Wonder of wonders, after Laura put her bitch on, the company rep hung up, fixed her problem with no more unplugging this or that, and called her back within 15 minutes to tell her the issue was resolved.

After she finished telling me the story, I congratulated her. After all, she is her mother's daughter, and it wasn't until she stopped being nice that her problem wasn't a problem anymore.

Does all of this mean there's no room for nice in our world? Not at all. But nice has become a trap, another word used to control women and our behavior. And it should never be confused with words like "kind," "generous," "thoughtful," "charitable," and others, all of which are far more definitive and therefore, accurate and welcome than the vague, often sinister "nice."

By all means, do good. Be thoughtful, be kind, be generous, be charitable. But be all of those things because you consciously choose to, not because you think you need to be "nice." Do not become a martyr to nice, turning into one of those simpering, put-upon women who runs around like a gerbil on a wheel, doing everything, running everything, and deflecting praise while taking on yet another project to garner more of the same. Because no matter how much those women do, no one likes them. They're annoying. They make the rest of us look bad, and they feed into the unattainable expectations the world sets for nice women. Should you know one of those women, please bitch-slap her for the rest of us. Should you be one of those women, STOP.

Don't be afraid to set boundaries. Saying, "No" does not mean you're a bad person. It means you're a sane person. One who recognizes the reality that trying to please everyone by being "nice" all of the time makes you unhappy, unproductive and the polar opposite of nice.

There is one notable exception to all of this. You are fully entitled to be nice to yourself. In fact, you should be, because if you don't treat yourself well, it's a good bet no one else will, either.

Being nice to ourselves is not something we're comfortable with, mostly because we don't feel we deserve it, which is really stupid. The woman who does everything for everyone else while serving herself last deserves nice more than anyone. But putting ourselves first and being nice to ourselves at least occasionally would mess with the status quo, which nice girls don't do.

So ironically, in order to be nice to yourself, you may also have to put on your bitchy-girl pants and claim some time for you, allowing everyone else to deal with their own stuff while you practice the highly enjoyable art of self-indulgence.

The upside to being nice to yourself, despite the objections of those you are temporarily "neglecting" while you care for yourself, is that you will indeed be happier, calmer, and ultimately more productive doing things that actually matter to you. You'll waste less time on things that you finally realize are better handled by someone, anyone, other than you.

This may not look nice to those around you, especially because you may be forcing them to deal with their own stuff while you, oh, I don't know, get a massage, drink some wine, buy some shoes, whatever. Too bad. Like every other word herein, it's all relative. They have their definition; you have yours.

So stop being so damn nice already. And if you must be nice, be nice to yourself and don't be afraid to get your bitch on once in a while. Sometimes, it's the nicest thing you can do for yourself.

Try This!

List five things you've done recently while trying to be "nice." Next to each item, write how you felt after you did it—happy, stressed, taken for granted, etc. Then, draw a line through each item that didn't make you feel great and DON'T DO IT AGAIN.

1._____

_____

2._____

_____

3._____

_____

4._____

_____

5._____

_____

Now, list five times when you had to get your bitch on—but you got something done. Next to each item, again write how you felt—empowered, confident, successful, etc.

1._____

_____

2._____

_____

3._____

_____

4._____

_____

5._____

_____

Finally, list five nice things you can do for yourself and a date by which you will treat yourself. Then DO THEM.

1._____

_____

2._____

_____

3._____

_____

4._____

_____

5._____

_____

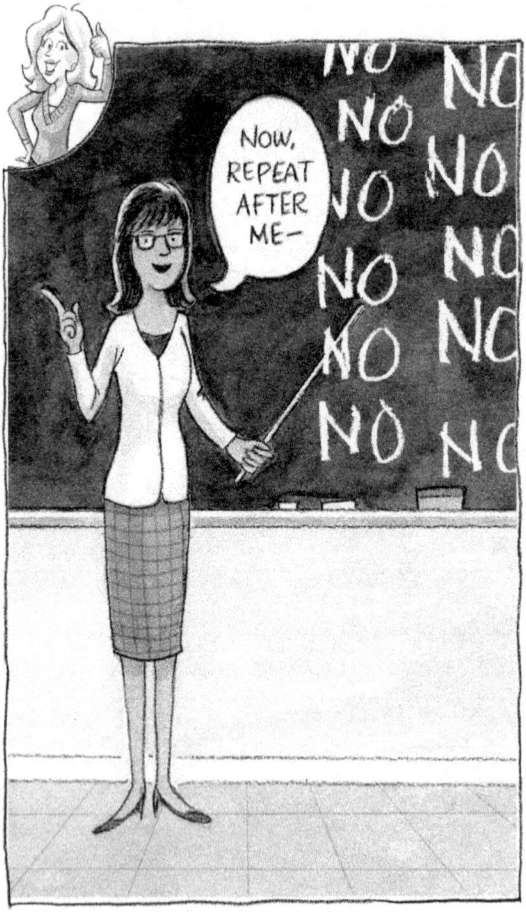
NOW, REPEAT AFTER ME–

Chapter 5

No

No

adverb

1. expression of a negative
2. refusal or denial of a request
3. in no way or not at all
4. not any
5. a rejection
6. disapproval
7. dissent

Look at that list of definitions. Seriously? Two letters. Who would ever think a word with two little letters could cause so much trouble? Yet, if there were ever a word to cause women endless consternation and anxiety, "no" is it.

I mean, look at the words associated with it: dissent, denial, refusal, not at all, a negative, to reject, to express disapproval of, can't. Those are two scary letters.

"No" packs a powerful punch. It's a word we women expect to be used against us, one which we use regularly against our kids (or so they believe), and yet one which we're afraid to use to protect ourselves.

"No" has its beginning in a woman's life as a safe word. Our parents use it to teach us what not to do in order to keep us out of trouble. "No, don't touch," "No, that's hot," "No, don't eat that," and so on.

But as we grow, "no" can be a weapon of sorts, used to keep girls, and later women, in check. In their place. A place determined by someone else, not the women in question. Historically, women were told "no" when they asked for the same rights as men. Women weren't allowed to own property, vote, or earn a wage equal to male counterparts. Thankfully, some of those issues have been resolved, but it's still an uphill battle for girls and women to hold onto equal footing, and "no" leads the charge against us.

It's a complicated word, too, for all of its brevity. Take, for example, the case of an eleven-year-old girl from Philadelphia who, in 2012, took on the Catholic Archdiocese of Philadelphia for kicking her off of her Catholic Youth Organization football team because she was a girl. The young lady objected to her dismissal, taking her case public and eventually receiving a reversal of the ruling.

Yet to some, the church's reasoning that her ejection from the sport was a safety issue gave the "no" some heft. After all, if it's about keeping a child safe, isn't "no" an appropriate response?

The biggest problem with the safety "no" is that it's frequently based on unfounded assumptions. Women are "the weaker sex," so it's society's (read: men's) job to keep women safe, to keep them from putting themselves at risk by doing something that's going to get them hurt, whether they want to do it or not.

Tell that "weaker" line to a woman whose children are threatened. Comparisons to a lioness when someone is threatening your kids are not unfounded, am I right? Or ask the young Virginia woman who, also in 2012, lifted a car off of her father when she found him pinned beneath it. If I found someone I loved stuck under a car, you're damn right I'd lift it up. Weak, my ass.

Okay, those may be exceptions to the fact that women are not physically as strong, in terms of pure muscle strength, as men. But to categorically restrict women to the sidelines (literally) because of their sex ignores the many other strengths women bring to any given situation, from flexibility, to endurance, to emotional fortitude.

That's the insidious power of "no." On the surface, it appears to be protecting us, when in reality, it's knocking us off our feet. Murky waters, indeed, and the implication of those two little letters can be powerful, whether spoken or merely implied, as is often the case in a culturally based "no."

Culturally based "no's" are usually silent, but can be more powerful than a "no" shrieked by a two-year old having a tantrum in the middle of a shopping mall. (Don't you hate it when that happens?)

In certain societies, "no" is used to keep women from gaining an education or meaningful employment. Then, "no" morphs into a silent weapon, as destructive as anything physical, undermining the very fabric of a society.

Those "no's" are particularly hard to challenge, as evidenced by the attacks on the women who do. Witness Malala Yousafzai, the young woman shot by the Taliban at age 15 for speaking out for girls' rights to an education in Pakistan. Thankfully, Malala survived and continues to inspire women to challenge the word "no" when it is used to deny them basic freedoms and rights.

Yet every term is relative, and while "no's" in other parts of the world have more overt and often dangerous consequences if challenged, in more "developed" countries, "no" can still be a weapon, whether used by a society's unspoken standards or used by we women ourselves, when we engage in self-talk.

Women are making progress, certainly. But when a woman as accomplished as Hillary Clinton (like her or not, she's an ambassador for women) jokes that the title of her memoir should be *"The Scrunchie Chronicles: 112 Countries and It's Still All about My Hair,"* well, it proves we still have a long way to go.

For many of us, the battle rages as much on the inside as the outside. How many times have you thought about doing something, anything, and thought, "Oh no, I couldn't do *that*," whatever "that" is. We gals are so good at limiting ourselves that it only takes two letters to bring us to a grinding halt.

Yet, oddly enough, the same word that stops us can be the very word that gets us moving again, provided we learn to use it to our advantage.

Saying "no" to the things and people who keep us from doing what we want, and getting where we want to go, can work for us as well as it's worked against us in the past. But first, we have to learn to say "no" to ourselves.

Sometimes, we gals just need a good talking to—inside of our own heads. As in *No, I won't accept that limitation. Just because I'm in my forties, or fifties or whatever, it doesn't mean I can't go to nursing school, or get my master's in business, or finally learn to speak Italian. My circumstances/life-choices/decisions even as recently as this morning don't have to dictate the rest of my life or even my day. So, no, I'm not giving up. I want something more.*

Am I oversimplifying? Maybe. But every change begins with a decision. Making that decision a declaration upon which you can then act crystalizes it and consequently gives it power.

But the power of "no" doesn't have to apply only to the big stuff. In fact, you'll never be able to even start to think about becoming a brain surgeon or an astronaut or a teacher or even a part-time office manager until you learn to use "no" to alter the most basic circumstances and time sucks in your life.

Remember our last dirty word, "nice"? One of the antidotes to crippling yourself by being too nice is to use the word "no." Use it to set boundaries. Use it to redefine who you are and what you're willing to put up with. Use it to help everyone else in your life learn to manage their own stuff, thereby extricating you from their lives and plopping you directly into your own, allowing you time to think about who you are and what you want.

Reflection isn't a word we use well in this country. We're too busy careening around from one "essential" task to another. Yet if we really think about it, a tremendous amount of what occupies our time is just stuff. Your time is worth more than that.

So reflect, already. Think about the big stuff, and how you've let "no's"—spoken or not—stop you. Then move on to the little things that eat up your precious 24 hours. Decide what you can say "no" to and do it.

It takes a brave woman to challenge a "no," and thank God they are out there. Otherwise, we'd all still be wearing aprons, a pearl choker, heels, and full makeup while making dinner, managing our kids, running a household with money that's assigned to cover expenses (but isn't ours) and greeting our man with a martini in a house he owns and we're just allowed to live in. (Some men out there would be just fine with that, believe me.)

But it's time to stop thinking that those brave women are just "out there." There's not a reason in the world that you can't challenge your own no's, and then say "no" right back to them. Think about what you want, where you want to be and what's holding you back.

Learn to say "no" to little things. If someone asks you to stop at the store, get gas in the car, throw in some laundry, and you don't want to, just say "no." Same thing with work. If it's not your boss asking you to do something, it's okay to say "no" if the request will take away from what's important to you.

You'll find the resulting freedom invigorating, not to mention transforming. Starting with the little things is the first step towards changing the big things.

Remember, too, that "no" is a complete sentence. How often do you try to say "no" to something, only to get tripped up by your endless need to explain and justify your answer? The more you talk, the less you convince not only everyone else, but yourself. Before you know it, you're committed to yet another thing you don't want to do.

Say "no" and then SHUT UP. Just stop talking. Unless you still live with your parents or you've barked a stressed out "NO!" at your boss, you don't owe anyone an explanation for choosing to do or not to do something. If you have to add more words, "No, I'm sorry. I can't," pretty much says everything that needs to be said without undermining the basic idea, which is "no."

It's time to take back the weapon, ladies, and use it to our advantage. Thoughtful deployment of those two little letters can change your life. So decide how you want to feel, how you want to live, and what you want to do and use "no" to help you get there.

And while you're at it, when you decide what you want, refuse to take "no" for an answer.

Try This!

List five things you've done recently that you didn't want to do. Look at each item and decide if it could have been handled by someone else. Then, write the sentence, "No, I can't do that," next to each item that should be someone else's responsibility (probably all of them) and say it out loud as you write. The next time you're asked to take on any of the items, respond with, "No, I can't do that."

1._____

_____

2._____

_____

3._____

_____

4._____

_____

5._____

_____

Next, list five things you've wanted to do but you let the word, "No" stop you (dance lessons, going back to school, etc.). Next to each item, write down why you didn't do what you wanted. Then, write down how you could have accomplished each thing. Finally, if it is still important to you, choose a date by which you will begin to work towards your goal and write down the date.

1._____
_____
_____
_____

2._____
_____
_____

3._____
_____
_____
_____

4. _____
_____
_____
_____
5. _____
_____
_____
_____

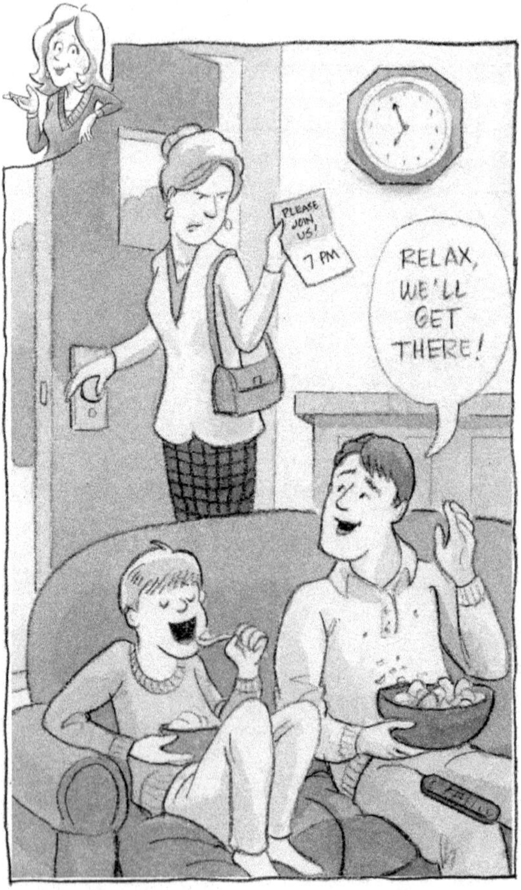

PLEASE JOIN US!
7 PM
RELAX, WE'LL GET THERE!

Chapter 6

Relax

Re·lax

verb

1. to make less tense or rigid
2. to ease up on, make less strict
3. to decrease force or effort
4. to make less severe
5. to relieve from worry or tension
6. to indulge in rest or recreation

"I don't know what you're getting so upset about. Will you *relax*?"

Did you just find yourself gritting your teeth and clenching your fists? Few words have the power to elicit a gut response in us that is as diametrically opposed to their intended use as the word "relax." Particularly if the word is being used by our husbands. Or our kids. Or anyone else who is not us and is telling us we should relax.

Relax is the word those closest to us use to let us know they think we're crazy. It's a word that has a bunch of other, invisible words right behind it.

Words like, "You're insane," or "You're acting like a psycho again."

Of course, the people accusing us of being over-reactive, wild-eyed nut jobs who make mountains out of molehills and stress everyone else out with our obsessive-compulsive demands that everything be done our way are the same people who will come running to us when everything goes to hell in a hand basket and expect us to fix it. Until then, though, they want us to RELAX.

"Relax" is code for "leave me alone." When your dear ones tell you to relax, they're really telling you to back off, shut up, and disappear. If someone has just smacked you with the word "relax," you've gotten under their skin and they want you to go away.

Usually, the reason you've annoyed them to the point that they lob "relax" in your direction is you're reminding them to do something they don't want to do, like clean up their stuff (applies to kids, husbands, and significant others), or start on some school work, or get showered and ready to go out because you're due at some event in a half hour and they're still on the couch, watching television and eating Doritos.

One of the challenges of being a woman is that we're usually the schedulers, the ones in charge of keeping track of where everyone has to be and then getting them there, dressed appropriately and with sharpened number two pencils, or a wrapped gift, or a plant for Mother's Day. We're supposed to do all of this with a team of reluctant players, none of whom want to be on the field or appreciate the time and effort we've put into executing the playbook. (Every once in a while, I come up with a well-placed sports metaphor. It still surprises me.)

When we're faced with our team's rebellion, especially when it comes in the form of ignoring our pleas to get going so many times that we've lost count, we get ugly. And yes, they deserve it. But they don't think they do. So after we've lost our minds and shrieked so loudly that the neighbor's dog starts howling, they look at us derisively and toss this chapter's opening line our way.

Once that shot has been fired, well, there's no going back, nor will there be any actual relaxing happening any time soon. Because what usually happens next is an escalation of shrieking, some door slamming, occasional swearing, and in my case, a run for my blood pressure medicine. Or an uncorked bottle of wine, whichever happens to be closer. (I don't drink as much as I pretend to. Really.)

To be sure, we women want to relax. I mean, who wouldn't, especially if you apply the definitions above and you can relax rules, making them less strict or severe, or bring relief from the effects of tension and anxiety? Who wouldn't want to relieve oneself from worry or tension?

And if we only had ourselves to worry about, I'm pretty sure we could do just that. It's when you throw families, friends, co-workers, in short, other people, into the mix, that relaxing becomes an elusive Holy Grail, forever to be chased, but never actually grasped.

Yet, entire industries have arisen in an effort to help us gals grab hold of relaxing. Yes, it sounds counter-productive, but the only way we can get some relaxation is to grab it. No one is gliding into relaxation; it's a free-for-all cage match to get your fair share. But back to the industrialization of relaxation. Think spas.

Back in our mothers' day, there was no such thing as a spa where a woman could go for a day of pampering, getting a massage, a facial and a manicure while wearing a fluffy robe, and being served a fruity drink, accompanied by soothing, piped in mood music.

Well, there were places where one could get a massage, but they were: a) usually in a back alley somewhere, b) not meant for women, and c) not really massages. At least not the kind of massage in which a woman was on the receiving end. Women were giving massages, for sure…well, you get the idea.

Further, anything called a spa back then was what we now call rehab. There were health benefits to be had, but they were usually of the medicinal, drying out variety.

In fact, the very idea of a massage sounds perverse to women of our mothers' generation. In their minds, massage = orgy, or something their husbands did overseas while they were at war—not something decent people even thought about. On those all-too-rare occasions when I actually go to a spa to get a massage, my mother's commentary runs along the lines of, "I don't know how you can do that. Letting strangers touch you when you don't have any clothes on—ugh!" (Don't knock it 'til you try it, Mom.)

Spas and women's retreats are big business these days. Everyone wants us to relax, especially if we have to hand them some of our hard-earned money to do it. If we have at least $150 we don't know what to do with, we can buy ourselves some of that relaxation stuff, assuming we aren't having a panic attack over the $150 part.

Yet, even if we decide we're worth it (and yes, we are), the very act of getting to the place where we're going to relax can often be so stress inducing, it makes the entire venture not worth the effort.

How many times have you tried to do something for yourself that in some way requires you to be absent from the home front? Do notice those words, "home front," because the planning required for most women to leave the house for more than a two hour stretch calls to mind a military maneuver. By the time a woman makes sure her kids and husband have transportation to wherever they're supposed to go, necessary uniforms and clothing are clean and wearable, her mother's doctor's appointment is rescheduled to a different day, there's food in the fridge for snacking as well as dinner prepared and ready to heat up, she's too exhausted to contemplate going anywhere aside from her own couch. Getting out is a battle, no question, and for many of us, it's tempting to quit while we're behind and ditch the whole idea.

Genuine relaxation borders on the mythical for many women. We've heard of it and it sounds like a great idea. It's just not real.

The main problem with the word relax, and our instinct to do the exact opposite after being instructed to "relax" by others, is the word's use as a passive-aggressive weapon. When someone shoots the "relax" arrow in your direction, it's an attempt to take your power. You are being dismissed. They're telling you that whatever it is you're concerned about or whatever you want them to do is not important.

That's the subliminal message in a nutshell. WHAT YOU WANT IS NOT IMPORTANT. Therefore, forget it, leave us alone and RELAX.

No wonder we explode. So how, then, do we disarm the bomb and embrace the word for what it is?

Communication is key. Of course, dissecting complicated family dynamics and providing individual solutions here isn't possible. But what is possible is for all of us to step back and look at how we're asking/demanding/begging for cooperation when it comes to getting our families, friends, co-workers, etc. to do stuff.

Clearly stating the goal and guiding everyone towards a specific course of action the first time you ask is essential. "Okay, listen up. The party starts at 2:00. We need to be in the car by 1:30. Showers have to start now. Who's going first?" Or, "When you've finished eating, rinse your plates off, put them in the dishwasher, and wipe off the table. Understood?"

Are clear, direct requests going to solve your problem? Hahahahaha! Of course not. But it's a start at getting your power back. Then, when no one does what you've asked, you can follow up with, "I've asked you to do XYZ. I know it's not important to you, but it is important to me and it needs to be done." Then stop talking and stare.

Staring is an underrated, highly effective means of getting things done, especially when accompanied by stony silence. We women talk so much that we're tuned out by our families, reduced to the "Wa-wa-wa-wa, wa-wa-wa-wa" voice of the adults from the Charlie Brown cartoons. Staring plus silence will usually result in one of two things —either they'll grudgingly get up and do what you want, or they will challenge you with a "Why do I have to do this now?" query, at which point you may respond, "Because I asked you to do it. And given everything I do for you, I think you can do this for me." Did I mention that guilt is a powerful means of getting things done, too?

The whole point here is to stave off the escalation in tensions that results in the dismissive "Will you just RELAX?" shot being fired. Every woman who has ever screamed at her family (read, all of us), knows how easy it is to find yourself in the middle of a shouting match without realizing how you got there. Trying to take control of the situation before it gets to that point allows you to likewise take control of the word relax and return it to its original meaning—one that will actually benefit you.

Which brings us back to spas.

If you should be so fortunate to have an opportunity to indulge in a spa day, or for that matter, any day that revolves around you relaxing in the true sense of the word, TAKE IT. Do not let everyone else's schedules, obligations, itinerary, or whatever keep you from taking advantage of time spent exclusively on you. I, personally, can count on one hand the number of times I've been to a spa, but oh, those were good days. And the memory, along with the anticipation of someday repeating the experience, has gotten me through many a tough moment.

And here's a newsflash: You don't have to make sure everyone else's stuff is handled before you walk out the door. In fact, if you really want to reclaim the word relax, leave others' stuff for them to handle. Abandoning everyone else's responsibilities serves two purposes—they take on their own responsibilities, and they get to see first-hand just how much you do for them.

So on your official relaxing day, DO NOT prepare meals, make sure everyone has their uniforms ready, or schedule transportation. Assuming we're talking about people who should be reasonably capable of managing their own stuff for a day, let them handle it, from soup to nuts.

BUT—and this is on you, ladies—know that it won't be done your way. That's okay, too. In fact, it's more than okay, because sometimes, in defense of all those telling us to back off and relax, we do get a bit crazy. Wild-eyed, compulsively crazy, which at least occasionally justifies their dismissive eye-rolling, sighing, and telling us to RELAX!

Remember, one of the definitions for relax is "to ease up on, make less strict." Translation: It doesn't have to be done your way, as long as it gets done. Loosening up on demands of "my way or the highway" will go far in keeping the peace and genuinely allowing us to relax, whether we're at the spa or staring at a sink full of dishes that haven't been put in the dishwasher just yet. Relaxation is a mindset—one to which we must set out minds and learn to live with.

So it follows that you don't really need to go to a spa to relax. You can find a way to truly relax in your own home, provided you're willing to let some stuff slide. It's okay to occasionally relax your standards and leave the dishes and the laundry. It's even okay to skip making dinner. Tell everyone you're taking the night off, pour yourself a glass of wine, pick up the latest copy of *MORE* or *In Style* magazines, plop yourself on the couch and relax. Let them eat cake, à la Marie Antoinette. Or cereal. Or whatever. Just *relax* and don't stew over it for one night.

Once you regain ownership of the word relax, you can use it the way it was meant to be used, "to relieve (yourself) from worry or tension," and perhaps even "indulge in rest or recreation."

Then, the next time someone in your inner circle tells you to relax, you can smile, take a deep breath, and say, "Thanks, I think I will." As you go about your business, leave them to theirs and let the chips—and if you're so inclined, the chocolate chip cookies you'll eat while relaxing—fall where they may.

Try This!

Think about the last time someone told you to "relax," when they clearly weren't suggesting you take a load off and have a piña colada. Write down the incident, as well as how it made you feel and why. Next, write down how you can handle similar situations differently to avoid future confrontations.

_____

_____

_____

_____

_____

_____

_____

_____

_____

_____

Now, write down five things that you would find truly relaxing. Think about how you could make at least three of them happen. Finally choose one of the activities and create a plan and a date for grabbing some relaxation for yourself.

1._____

2._____

3._____

4._____

5._____

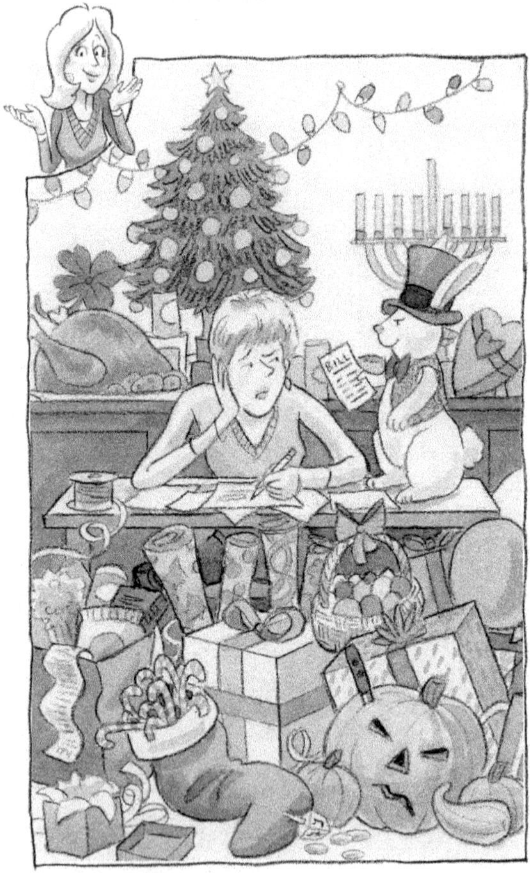
BILL

Chapter 7

Holidays

Ho·li·days

noun

1. a day or days when people are exempt from work
2. a period of seasonal celebration between Halloween and New Year's Day
3. a time of rest
4. a day or season grounded in religious and familial obligations and traditions

The Twelve Days of the Season
(Sung to the tune of *The Twelve Days of Christmas*)

On the first day of the season, a thought occurred to me: I'm stepping headlong into misery.

On day two of the season, a thought occurred to me: This mall is really crowded, and I'm stepping headlong into misery.

On day three of the season, a thought occurred to me: I've addressed a hundred cards, this mall is really crowded, and I'm stepping headlong into misery.

On day four of the season, a thought occurred to me: The tree lights just went out, I've addressed a hundred cards, this mall is really crowded, and I'm stepping headlong into misery.

On day five of the season, a thought occurred to me: I HATE BAKING COOKIES! The tree lights just went out, I've addressed a hundred cards, this mall is really crowded, and I'm stepping headlong into misery.

On day six of the season, a thought occurred to me: I've overspent my credit, I HATE BAKING COOKIES! The tree lights just went out, I've addressed a hundred cards, this mall is really crowded, and I'm stepping headlong into misery.

*On day seven of the season, a thought occurred to me: Where are those *#%! boxes? I've overspent my credit, I HATE BAKING COOKIES! The tree lights just went out, I've addressed a hundred cards, this mall is really crowded, and I'm stepping headlong into misery.*

*On day eight of the season, a thought occurred to me: There's no more wrapping paper, where are those *#%! boxes? I've overspent my credit, I HATE BAKING COOKIES! The tree lights just went out....*

*On day nine of the season, a thought occurred to me: I'm sick of Christmas carols, there's no more wrapping paper, where are those *#%! boxes? I've overspent my credit....*

On day ten of the season, a thought occurred to me: Whose idea was eggnog? I'm sick of Christmas carols, there's no more wrapping paper, where are those *#%! boxes?....

On day eleven of the season, a thought occurred to me: The dog just ate the manger, whose idea was eggnog? I'm sick of Christmas carols, there's no more wrapping paper....

On day twelve of the season, a thought occurred to me: I've gained seven pounds, the dog just ate the manger, whose idea was eggnog? I'm sick of Christmas carols, there's no more wrapping paper, where are those *#%! boxes? I've overspent my credit, I HATE BAKING COOKIES! The tree lights just went out, I've addressed a hundred cards, this mall is really crowded... AND I'M STEPPING HEADLONG INTO MISERY!!!!!

Who says I don't have any Christmas cheer?

Truth is, I used to have a lot of it, back when my kids were young and their little eyes would shine with Christmas wonder. And Halloween wonder. And Thanksgiving wonder. And Easter wonder. And wonder for every single holiday it was my job to make wondrous.

But after years...make that decades...of being the keeper of all things holiday, I'd just as soon trade my figgy pudding for bottle of wine and a plane ticket to a beach—return date open-ended.

That would actually be a holiday, or a time of rest, as one definition notes. What's become known as "The Holidays" are anything but restful for a woman, unless you count collapsing in exhaustion after a seven hour trip to the mall, usually on top of a pile of wrapping paper with Dollar Store bows stuck to your cheeks.

Or think of National Lampoon's classic film, *Christmas Vacation*. You have to laugh at Clark Griswold's excessive efforts to create the perfect holiday for his family, replete with 25,000 lights stapled to the roof of his house and a Christmas tree so huge it blew out the living room windows when Clark cut the binding rope.

Hahahahaha! That Clark sure was a funny guy. Until Clark's Christmas madness became our norm. Bigger, better, and more, more, more, or it isn't even worth doing.

As is our American tendency, we go a little overboard with holidays. Overboard as in the difference between the QE II and a fishing dinghy. Regardless of your holiday of choice (or punishment —you decide), it's a safe bet that wherever you may have started on the scale of holiday madness, you're now firmly rooted in months-long where-are-the-giant-blow-up-lawn-decorations, when-shall-we-host-the-gingerbread-house-decorating-party-for-the-entire-neighborhood, have-to-go-back-to-the-mall-for-the-eighty-seventh-time, out-of-fried-onions-for-the-damn-green-bean-casserole, may-have-to-miss-a-mortgage payment mayhem.

Are we having fun, yet?

It would be one thing if all of this excess made a permanent impression. But I dare you to ask any one of your children to name more than one of their Christmas gifts from last year. Sure, if you bought them a car or a new computer or an Xbox (which, by the time of this publication will probably be obsolete), they might have a vague recollection. Anything else? Fuhgeddaboudit—because they have.

Lest it seem that I'm making our kids out to be ungrateful wretches, take the challenge yourself. What did you receive last Christmas? Go on, I dare you to name three things. Better yet, what did you give anyone? All those hours upon hours trudging through the mall or trolling the Internet in your pajamas and bunny slippers at 1 a.m. because you got caught doing it at work and need to shop in the middle of the night since you don't have any other time—can you remember what you bought *anyone*?

And let's not even talk about the money. Because even sensible people go insane at Christmas. My husband, who is not a believer in extravagant gift giving, routinely asks what I'm buying for the "kids" (all adults now) and pronounces it "not enough," whereupon he proceeds to go out and buy more stuff, which they won't remember, to put under the tree.

Of course, Christmas isn't the only culprit, not by a long shot. The Halloween season (every holiday is a season, now) starts at the end of August as pumpkins offer goofy grins next to back-to-school-supplies. Costumes, which used to consist of a plastic mask and a cheap polyester outfit bought from Kmart, now require elaborate blueprints and copious amounts of time and parental involvement to construct, not to mention copious amounts of money to finance.

Should you opt to encourage a simple costume—whatever happened to being a ghost in a white sheet or a "bum" using dad's old clothes?—prepare for looks of pity from the parents who turned their young one into a live action transformer robot (sure, it was a really cool costume), or an actual ringing cell phone. Congratulations; in your efforts to rein in the madness, you've created your own Charlie Brown, who will probably come home with a bag full of rocks.

Even Thanksgiving, with its deceptively simple emphasis on a bountiful harvest, is not simple anymore. You're either painstakingly recreating every three-hour-prep-time, seven-hour-cook-time dish your grandmother ever served, or conversely studying the Food Network for new recipes utilizing farro, quinoa, or some other ingredient you've never heard of. Then you have to plan a fancy "tablescape" involving scores of dishes, glassware, table runners, gourds, leaves, and pumpkins. Finally, don't forget to concoct a unique cocktail for the day's festivities. Because if you don't, well, who cares? Then it's just another dinner with a turkey on the table.

Of course I could go on (I can *always* go on), but any festivity termed a "holiday" these days translates into mountains of extra work, time, and money—and the burden is almost solely on the shoulders of the woman of the house. (Unless you live with your own version of Clark Griswold, in which case I say, God help you.)

It starts with the best of intentions. Women initiate traditions (which by the way, should be defined as the never-ending practice of doing the same things over and over until a stint in an asylum begins to look like a vacation) as a balm to provide comfort and continuity during special times in a family's life. But over time, even the shiniest of traditions can tarnish, either because they're increasingly complicated to execute or because they're mind-numbingly boring. But the simple fact that something has been declared a tradition enshrines it in a kryptonite enclosed coffer that even Superman couldn't break through.

Just try not to decorate the house with thousands of twinkle lights this year. I dare you.

Actually, I do dare you.

If you're ever going to be free of the never-ending holiday life sentence, ladies, you'll have to be brave.

The masses will howl with protest: "Whaddaya mean we're not going to bake seven varieties of pie for Thanksgiving?!" "But we *have* to put up the collection of forty-five light-up houses in the Christmas display!" "Where are the roasted pumpkin seeds from the half dozen jack-o-lanterns you always carve?"

Stand firm, girls. Extricating yourself from this lunacy will not be easy. But it can be done.

You have several options: Run away and join the circus, which would be redundant, as you already live in one, or make gradual changes to your particular brand of madness until you can think about a holiday without having to put your head between your knees and breathe into a paper bag.

First of all, you must steel yourself to resist. Refuse to be sucked in too early. Jack-o-lanterns don't surface before October, turkeys before November, or Christmas trees before December. And I personally could do without the parade of Easter chicks and bunnies altogether, but that's just me. It's time we took back the calendar from the marketers who would have us stringing Christmas lights at the end of August.

Second, tone down the decorating. I mean, how are you supposed to clean around all of that crap four or five months out of the year? Subscribe to the "less is more" mantra. Keep your favorite decorations handy—thus avoiding the attic and basement foraging that inevitably results in bumps, bruises, and the need for a shower—and put a few items around the house that will call to mind the next holiday without smothering everyone in it.

If you have really insistent balkers on this one, lay down the law: Anyone who wants to decorate with a profusion of crap must help put it up, clean around it for the duration and help take it down. No negotiating.

You can also start to set aside decorating items to "gift" to your kids or others, if they want them, that is, which they probably don't. During a period of insanity years ago, I purchased not one, but two sets of light-up villages, compete with little trees, people, and accessories to make the scene more "realistic." Every year since, for decades, I hauled each little house and tiny figure out of its multi-layered packaging (God forbid anything breaks; I should be so lucky), and set them up around my home. My intention was always to give one set to each of my daughters. (I started my son on a nutcracker collection which has also reached epic numbers.)

When I proposed my plan, my older daughter, Laura, looked at me and said, "I don't want to have to put up all that stuff and store it when I get a house." When I responded with, "I don't care; you're getting them anyway," Laura said, "Well you can give them to me, but the only way I'm putting them up is still in the box with the picture facing out." So much for tradition.

Which brings me to the next point. Don't assume that everyone is as attached to your traditions as you think, especially if you demand their cooperation in executing them. Kids, especially the adult kind who have their own stuff to handle, become noticeably less tied to something if they're called into service to make it happen. Try saying, "Hey, I'll bake nine different kinds of Christmas cookies this year if you'll give me a weekend and help me." You'll be amazed at how suddenly everyone is on a diet.

If they do want to come and help you, bravo. Take the opportunity to spend some time with your family and immerse yourself in what all of this nonsense is really supposed to be about—love, and family, and all that stuff. Yet don't be afraid to scuttle some things altogether. Twenty-somethings DO NOT need Easter baskets.

When your kids do finally leave the nest (hey, it could happen), whatever you do, don't be one of those annoying women who insists that they spend every holiday with you doing what your family always did. Let them find their own way and start their own traditions. Perhaps take the opportunity to start a different gathering—maybe a casual one, like pizza on paper plates—and begin a new tradition that's less work and more fun for everyone, especially you.

And by all means, get a handle on the money thing. The amount of money spent on all things holiday in this country is borderline obscene. Set aside a reasonable amount for gifts, food, and decorations and stick to it. While you're at it, set a limit on gift giving as well. Better yet, if you and your loved ones don't need anything, donate to a charity and once again, recall what all of this is really supposed to be about.

Lastly, build mini-holidays into all of this madness for yourself. When you're out elbowing your way through crowds, standing seventh in line at the "Service Desk," and rifling through your purse for coupons that won't work for the items you want to buy, take a break. Sit at the food court and eat something bad for you, like ice cream for lunch. Or buy yourself some jewelry or a handbag with one of those stupid coupons. If you must suffer, at least give yourself a small reward for doing so.

It's impossible to feel festive when you're feeling frazzled. Pare down, scale back, regain your common sense, and rest. If you need a little help, I highly recommend sipping on some wine and munching store-bought goodies while snuggling with your grown-up kids, watching *How the Grinch Stole Christmas*, followed by *A Charlie Brown Christmas*, followed by *Rudolph the Red Nosed Reindeer*, followed by sharing memories, giggling, and refusing to gift wrap anything.

Now that's a holiday.

Try This!

Make a list of up to ten things you do repeatedly every holiday season that have become traditions to your family (making gingerbread houses, baking Thanksgiving pies, crafting an annual holiday poem—and if you do that, please stop). Next, put a + sign next to each item you WANT to continue and a – sign next to each thing you'd gladly tie a rock around and throw into the ocean. Finally, look at each item you've decided to continue and write one way you could simplify that tradition. ("Get help" should be next to EVERYTHING!)

1._____

2._____

3._____

4._____

5._____

6._____

7._____

_____

8._____

_____

9._____

_____

10._____

_____

Think about your holiday decorating. Below, list at least five items you could toss or give to someone. As each holiday arrives and passes, get rid of anything that sheds parts, looks like the dog chewed on it, or takes more than two minutes to unpack and assemble. Continue this new "tradition" until decorating takes no more than an hour or so. Use the additional time to drink wine and eat chocolate or store-bought cookies.

1._____

2._____

3._____

4._____

5._____

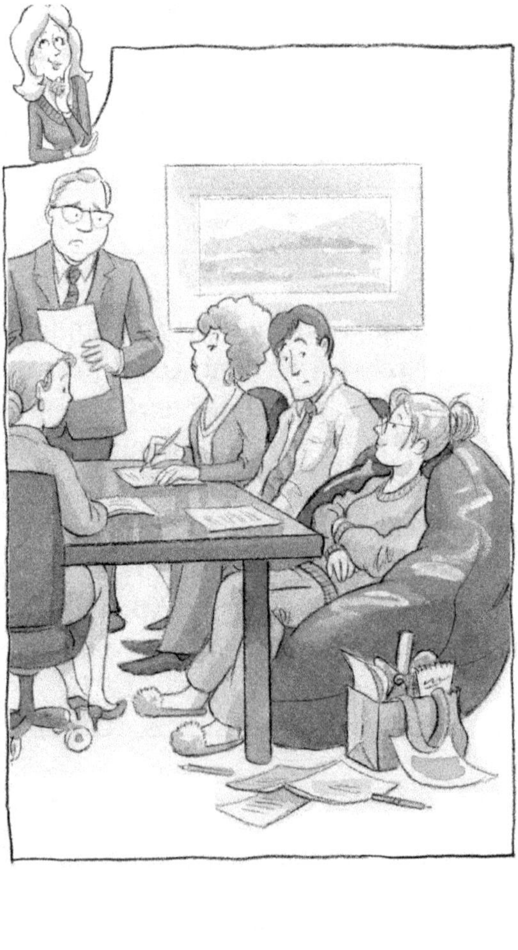

Chapter 8

Comfortable

Com·for·ta·ble

adjective

1. providing or producing physical or mental ease
2. being in a state of contentment and comfort
3. easy to be with or around; undisturbed

Ahhhh, comfort.

It's what we women long for. It's what we strive for. It's what we deserve.

So let's embrace the word and get comfortable already, right?

Wrong.

As with every word herein, "comfortable" is a sneaky little bugger. On the surface, it's all warm and fuzzy, all, "Yeah, let's snuggle." But dig a little deeper? More quicksand. The more you get caught in it and struggle to get out, the farther in you sink.

Comfortable is like one of those giant bean bag chairs that molds itself to your butt. You sit in it, scooch around a bit and before you know it, you're one with the chair. You can't move, and you certainly can't get up. It's captivatingly comfortable, until it isn't comfortable any more, but there's nothing you can do about it. You're stuck.

Yet, given what our days (and nights) are usually like, it's no wonder we women chase comfortable. At the end of a long day spent working, caring for families, and generally keeping up with the business of life, we can't wait to ditch our public personas, along with our public wardrobes, made-up faces and all, and get comfortable.

The result may not be pretty, but that's kind of the point. When we're ready to get comfortable, we aren't thinking pretty. We're thinking sweats, fuzzy slippers, and the TV remote, along with a giant jug of wine and copious amounts of chocolate.

I've been there. In fact, I go there often. Which is fine—most of the time. But as with just about anything, too much of a good thing usually isn't good. Getting too comfortable, in any number of areas, is a dangerous thing for women. It's what makes "comfortable" a dirty word.

At various times in a woman's life, comfortable is everything. As kids, we're all about comfortable; it's pretty much all that matters to a child, boy or girl. But as girls grow, we start comparing ourselves to unattainable standards of beauty, something men never do, and comfortable takes a back seat to pretty, which is precisely when things get decidedly uncomfortable for us.

From the time we first tweeze an eyebrow or nick ourselves shaving a delicate underarm, comfortable we aren't. We may be pretty, but with all it takes to get there and stay there, comfortable becomes a memory—reserved for pajama parties with our girlfriends where we try other beauty regimens, which are totally uncomfortable, and we're right back where we started.

During those adolescent years, we get comfortable in secret, at times and in places when we can be in hiding and no one save our immediate families and most trusted friends can ever see us as we really are. Then, comfortable may feel wonderful, but heaven forbid one of our brother's friends happens to catch us in our comfortable state—we're horrified, embarrassed, and about as uncomfortable as a girl can be.

So comfortable becomes a rarefied state, indulged in under the strictest of conditions, which is pretty much the antithesis of what comfortable means.

Then, we do a weird about-face. As life gets more complicated, and as many of us marry and have children, comfortable becomes our uniform. Not so much because we want it to, but because it's often all we can manage.

I vividly remember standing in my kitchen one day shortly after my first child was born, staring at the clock, which read 2 p.m., still in my pajamas and robe, hair unwashed, no makeup—I'm pretty sure I'd brushed my teeth, but even that was a crapshoot most days—and thinking, "Oh my God, I'm never going to be human again." When I finally managed to pull on sweatpants and a t-shirt (there was no attempt at a bra), I was actually proud of myself.

During those years, I saw myself in every young mom I encountered who stumbled through her day in a variation of my wardrobe—sloppy pants and food-stained shirts—while we tried to keep track of our kids and our sanity.

Needless to say, pretty was no longer a consideration, but comfortable was a sentence. Yet, we aspired to nothing more. If the shirt happened to be clean, well, that was good enough for us.

And here's where it starts to get tricky. Because we were so overworked and stressed, we resented the mere idea that we had to look presentable. We felt lousy about ourselves but we were too exhausted to do anything about it. In fact, wearing comfortable (if borderline disgusting) clothing was almost a badge of honor—proof that we were doing our jobs. It also meant that if we were lucky enough to be able to grab a nap during the day, there was no need to change our clothes. Which many of us didn't. Even at bedtime.

So we stuck with comfortable, even if it meant that we couldn't bear to look at ourselves in the mirror, which we obviously were not. But it was just easier that way.

While some of us had to snap out of it of necessity—anyone who returned to work outside of the home found most working environments frown on the dumpster-diver look in the office—some of us stayed in the land of comfortable, venturing out only on holidays and special occasions, and then only if we could still pull on a pair of pants with an elastic waist.

All of which is what makes "comfortable" a downright filthy word.

At the risk of repeating myself (see *Not Ready for Granny Panties, The 11 Commandments for Avoiding Granny Panties*, Chapter 7, "Thou Shalt Not Wear Elastic Waist Pants"), this bears repeating.

Ladies, unless you are carrying around an infant who is regularly throwing up on your shoulder (grandchildren don't count), unless you are sick, or unless you are actually engaged in an activity that requires rubber gloves and bleach, there is no excuse to walk around looking like you just got finished cleaning the bathroom.

While I will spare you my unsolicited fashion advice (really, see Chapter 7 of *Not Ready for Granny Panties, The 11 Commandments for*

Avoiding Granny Panties, there's plenty of it there), suffice it to say there are countless wardrobe options that allow a woman to look pulled together with minimal restrictions. In other words, you might not be sloppy sweats, ready-to-nap comfy, but you can be relatively comfortable and look like you didn't choose your outfit from the hamper.

For too many women, comfortable has become synonymous with "I don't give a damn." Yet lots of ladies feel like they've earned the right to be comfortable all of the time, and I don't disagree.

What I do disagree with is the idea that comfortable equals slovenly. It doesn't.

You deserve better than that. Every woman does. So throw out all of your comfortable clothes that look like they came from the costume department of *Les Miserables*, and buy yourself some things that fit—think spandex!—that make you feel good about yourself. While you're at it, get a new hair style and swipe on some lipstick.

Investing a little time and money in your appearance will make you feel comfortable in the most important of ways: in your own skin. And that's the best kind of comfortable of all.

But attire isn't the only area where women embrace and then are entrapped by "comfortable." Sometimes, that really comfy pair of sweats that we don't ever want to take off is the pair we wear in our heads, the one that keeps us from trying anything new, learning, or growing because we're so comfortable right where we are.

This trap opens for us at about the same time we start permanently living in our comfortable clothes—with the advent of motherhood. Once we're charged with the safe-keeping of a child, anything that smacks of the unknown is often viewed with fear and loathing.

That's especially true when we realize that kids like routine, and for a sleep-deprived, exhausted, stressed-out woman, keeping to a child's routine, particularly when it involves napping, is not only comfortable, it's of paramount importance. Did you ever just put your baby down for a nap only to have a well-meaning friend ring the doorbell as soon as you hit the bottom step? Many a friendship teeters on the precipice of extinction in that moment.

Our comfortable routines multiply exponentially as years pass and we're charged with getting everyone where they're supposed to be, including our husbands and ourselves. Any deviation from the routine can throw off the logistics for an entire neighborhood, especially if carpooling is involved, so it's essential that order be maintained. And while none of this involves comfort in the traditional sense of the word, make no mistake, there is an ease that comes things working the way they've been designed to.

So we cling to our comfortable routines, in the not-so-mistaken belief that they are what get us through the day. When what's expected to happen happens, well, we're comfortable. Not necessarily delighted or happy, but comfortable. Which is often enough, so there's no thought of breaking our patterns or habits.

Yet, those kid-filled years are also the ones when you look with longing at a new play opening at the theater, the release of a movie that you'd like to see that doesn't involve singing animals, or a restaurant you'd like to try that doesn't have chicken nuggets first on the menu. You tell yourself, "Someday. Someday I'll be able to see an R-rated movie again and eat a meal out without being surrounded by video games and talking animatronic characters. Someday."

When the kids eventually leave home (at least I think that's what's supposed to happen—I'm still waiting), "someday" arrives. It's finally time to get out there and DO stuff. And for many of us, the movies, the theater, and the restaurants, let alone anything more exciting…never happen.

Why? Because we're comfortable. We're also still tired. Tired from years of running, worrying, taking care of other people's stuff. So when we finally don't have to do that anymore, well, there's a certain appeal to sitting on the couch, remote in hand, and simply vegging out.

But do you know what happens to vegetables that hang around too long? They start to rot. Pretty soon, you're left with a smelly, disgusting mess that needs to be removed from the fridge with a hazmat suit and thrown into the garbage. Not that I'm comparing anyone to rotting vegetables. Well, not entirely.

Our reluctance to get on with things is often due to the residual feeling that change is bad. Change messes with the routine, which wreaks havoc with the schedule, which causes things to be left undone, which makes everyone cranky, etc., etc.

Years spent trying to maintain a schedule can leave a mark on a woman. More like a psychic scar. When finally freed from that burden, who could blame a gal for just wanting to sit on the couch, trying to decide whether to watch a *Say Yes to the Dress* marathon or sit through *Love Actually* for the fourteenth time? Parking yourself on the couch is a safe option. It's an easy option. It's also the option that soon makes your butt look like that bean bag chair you just can't seem to get out of.

"Comfortable," when used as an excuse to remain stationary, quickly translates into stale, which is what life becomes when we refuse to get out of our—granted, hard-won—comfort zones and get on with the fun of living when we finally have the chance.

Assuming we're willing to take the chance, that is.

For many women, being perpetually "on-call" is the biggest comfort zone of all. It's what we're used to. We've been everyone's "go-to" for decades; isn't that what we're supposed to be, and do, forever? Isn't there something in our unwritten job description that says, "for life" in the fine print?

Yes and no. Of course you're going to be there for your family. Forever and for always. But forever and for always does not translate into sitting around, waiting for the phone to ring to see who you have to save next. Once the kids move out (and if they refuse to move out, once they're out of college), it's time to hang up your superhero cape.

It's time to let everyone else start to handle their own stuff, which will, of course, make them extremely uncomfortable. But that's what's supposed to happen. Only it won't, if you won't let it. You need to get comfortable with the idea that it's not your job to solve everyone's every problems. They need to get comfortable with the idea that now, for the most part, it's on them because you need a life. (Prepare yourself for wide-eyed disbelief, at least initially, as your family wraps their collective heads around this concept.)

Once you free yourself from the need to be permanently available to your see to your family's every whim, you can think about trying something new, something that you've always wanted to try, and then you can face up to another kind of uncomfortable.

It follows that whenever we try something different, whenever we institute a change, there's a period of discomfort. The unknown has been the monster in the closet for so long that we have a knee-jerk reaction to kick away anything out of the ordinary—anything that would make us uncomfortable.

And that's okay. But stepping into those uncomfortable waters is precisely what we need to do to re-enter the land of the living. That place where grown-ups do those interesting things. Things that require thought, and yes, a little effort. Things that might be a little intimidating because of unknowns, but if attempted, might actually be fun—another word we treat with suspicion.

Just dip your toes in at first. Sign up for a class. Join a book club. Even trying a new restaurant can open the door to new adventures, especially if you're really feeling wild and try an entirely new cuisine.

Being comfortable, while it may sound great, can be treacherous territory for a woman. Be suspicious of it, especially if you start applying it as a barometer to multiple areas in your life, including your wardrobe and all of your leisure time. Use it sparingly, and know that a lack of comfort isn't always a bad thing.

Each of us has a different comfort threshold. The important thing is to challenge your particular comfort zone and step (you can leap, but only if you're ready) over it. Before you know it, you'll look forward to being uncomfortable, realizing that the unknown can lead to new adventures, new friendships and new joys.

That's worth being uncomfortable and hoisting yourself out of that bean bag chair any day.

Try This!

Get a large trash bag. Go to your closet and take out all of your comfortable clothes. Choose two pairs of sweatpants and three sweatshirts which you will wear only when you are sick, cleaning, or shoveling snow. Put the remainder in the trash bag. (The underprivileged do not want your old sweats. And do not put them in the laundry room under the premise that you'll use them as rags. You know you'll put them back in your closet.)

Next, do the same thing with your old, disgusting sneakers, mismatched socks, and undergarments with holes or stretched out elastic.

Finally, write the words "I will not look like a slob just to be comfortable" five times below. When you are finished writing, take the filled trash bag OUT TO THE TRASH.

1._____

_____

2._____

_____

3._____

_____

4._____

_____

5._____

_____

Now, write five things below that you've been talking about doing but haven't gotten your butt off the couch to do because you're too comfortable at home (see a play, go into the city for dinner, take a class). Choose at least three items and write down a date by which you will do them.

1._____
2._____
3._____
4._____
5._____

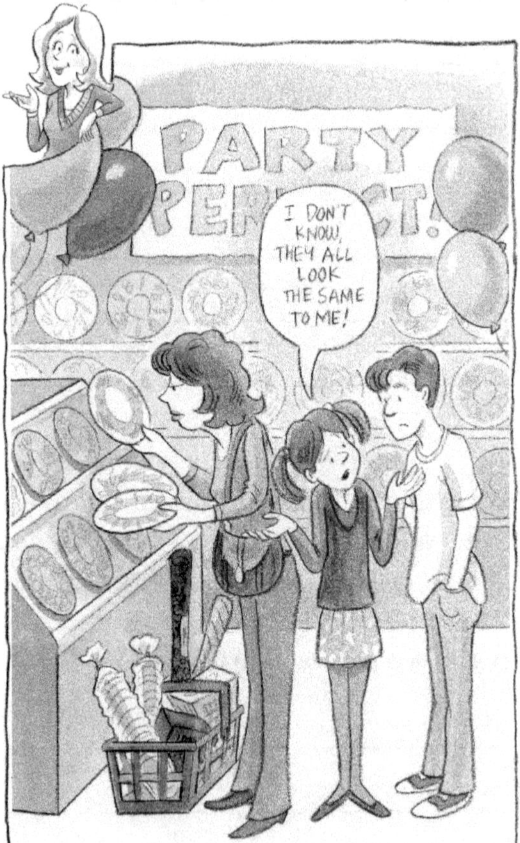
PARTY PER
CT!
I DON'T KNOW. THEY ALL LOOK THE SAME TO ME!

Chapter 9

Fine

Fine

adjective

1. good, acceptable, or satisfactory
2. excellent in quality and/or appearance

"Fine" is a fine word. In fact, it's even better than a fine word. Because before we dumbed it down to mean "okay," fine meant a thing of high quality—think "fine wine." But we women often take fine and turn it into "meh." It's as if when something is just "fine," it's not really what we want, but we'll put up with it.

So then the question becomes, what's wrong with that?

The trend of late decrees that everything must be described in terms of superlatives. As in, "OMG, it was the best, the most amazing, the most incredible, the most fabulous" whatever. Anything less barely registers, and heaven forbid whatever it is should be simply "fine." That all but equates to horrible, or embarrassing—anything but good.

Partially to blame are sites like Pinterest, with one-upmanship built into every post. It reminds me the old song lyric, "Anything you can do, I can do better. I can do anything better than you!" Pinterest is the visual manifestation of that.

It begins innocently enough, when an unsuspecting woman types the word "party" in the Pinterest search box. She thinks that perhaps she can get some cute ideas for a gathering she's hosting at her home. But there is no "cute" on Pinterest. There is only outrageous, over-the-top, out of control madness, where every party worth attending must have custom-made decorations that include thousands of twinkle lights, several hundred of which are somehow embedded in the table linens, multiple seven-tiered hors d'oeuvre stations, and color-themed cocktails garnished with fresh fruit carved in the shape of flowers and birds.

And let's not forget enshrining the party with images uploaded to Instagram, where any picture can be improved via filters to make whatever was actually there look better than it was in reality. The message is that no matter how good anything is, no matter how fabulous, expensive, and outrageous, we can still tweak it even further—effectively turning it into a fantasy that never existed in the first place.

When did the middle of the road disappear? What's wrong with things being okay, or good enough? If something can't be described as "awesome!" it's hardly worth doing any more. I mean, isn't anybody besides me sick of the word, "awesome!"? (And yes, it always has an exclamation point, or several, attached.)

I'm personally guilty of playing the "awesome" card. Now that I'm regularly involved on social media (which I loathe, I might add), I feel compelled to offer everyone who posts a picture, relates an event, or simply tells what they had for lunch the now-requisite, "Wow, that's awesome!" by way of acknowledgement. Let me note that most of the time, there's not much about any of it that's awesome.

All of this has the effect of rendering everything I say null and void by virtue of sameness and over-exposure, and also makes me sound like an idiot or a Valley Girl, which are kind of the same thing. Yet I'm hardly alone. Next time you're on Facebook, count how many times you read the word "awesome!"

Yet, were I to be totally honest in my commentary and dub something "nice," or "good," or the now-mediocre, "fine," I'd likely be blocked by every "friend" I have and reported to the social media powers that be for abuse due to lack of superlatives.

We've come to equate fine with another F-word—failure. If it's not awesome, epic, or amazing, then it's a big, fat fail. That's simply ridiculous. The idea that every event, every experience, every moment has to reach some kind of resounding crescendo to be worth anything is not only impossible, it's exhausting.

It simply can't be done. But that won't keep us from trying, by god.

At a recent family baby shower, I was asked to provide paper products—plates, cups, napkins, etc. Inherent in that is the concept that everything I purchased was intended to be used and then thrown away. Nothing was ending up in anyone's china cabinet to be tenderly placed on the table at holiday dinners and passed down for generations.

Anything I brought that would have held food and beverages would have been fine. But because I didn't want to disappoint anyone (I'm not sure who), I trucked to five stores, scoured multiple Internet sites and lost sleep at night worrying over those damn plates and cups. Ultimately, I ended up buying three different varieties and patterns of paper products and napkins in an effort to match the theme of the gathering. Which I did not. And no one cared. Except me.

I cared a lot. I didn't want to be the person who settled for fine. The result? I almost lost sight of the entire intention of the occasion, to celebrate the birth of a baby. Fortunately, a little spiked punch (yes, guys, we ladies always spike our punch at bridal and baby showers) snapped me out of it, as did the sight of my carefully purchased plates covered with food, as they were intended to be, the pattern I'd so diligently searched for invisible beneath the meal. Then, of course, the plates were dumped in the trash, which sealed the deal.

The plates were indeed fine. They were nice; they served their purpose; time to move on. Now think for a minute. How many ultimately inconsequential things have you obsessed over because you were being held hostage by the need for superlatives?

On any given day, at any time, we women can be called on to somehow contribute to something, whether taking part in a project at work, bringing a dish to a family gathering, or even providing plates for a party. While every experience needs to be evaluated on its own merit, it's safe to say, if you're a conscientious, intelligent person, whatever you do WILL BE FINE.

Which is okay. And nice. And good enough.

Keep in mind the whole point of whatever enterprise you're undertaking and your part in the same. Over the top is not always better, especially if other people are involved. If you get a little crazy and always outshine everyone else, you'll soon get a reputation for being that annoying woman who tries to out-do everybody. People will smile to your face, but they won't like you. No one likes that woman.

Embrace "fine." In fact, aspire to it. That way, you'll know whatever you're doing, it's more than good enough. Should you want to throw in a little extra effort occasionally, that's okay, but as long as fine is your benchmark, you can rest assured that you've done your job and for a change maybe even step back to enjoy whatever it is you're involved in.

While you're at it, impose at least a temporary personal ban on superlatives. Take the pressure to be awesome off your plate. Let the other hamsters spin on their wheels chasing the impossible and just give yourself a break. Once you release yourself from constantly chasing awesome, you may find you can actually cut back on the Prozac. If nothing else, you'll finally be well rested because, like I said, trying to be amazing is exhausting.

Now, before we leave fine entirely, a brief word of caution. As with any yin, there is always a yang. So it is with fine. While most of us spend our days chasing after some unattainable personal best in everything, exhausting ourselves in the process, there are those of us already so beaten down, so tired of trying, that "fine" becomes an excuse. An excuse to not give a damn.

For these gals, fine is synonymous with "Who cares?" because they don't.

Have you ever heard a tired woman say something along the lines of, "Oh, don't worry about it; it's fine," with resignation bordering on disgust in her voice? The fact is that whatever she's talking about is most definitely *not* fine, she's just too beat to put any effort into making it better. She's become used to settling for less than. That's not okay.

And let's not forget the times we use "fine" as a passive-aggressive weapon. You know, when your partner has done something that really pisses you off, but when he asks you if you're okay, you respond, "Yeah, I'm FINE."

First, you're not fooling anyone. You know you're not fine and he most certainly knows you're not fine, even though he will let the matter drop rather than set himself up for target practice—as the target. This one is our fault, ladies. You can't say you're fine when you're not, and then get mad at someone when they don't pursue the matter to try and figure out what you really mean.

In these cases, a reality check is in order. For you. When you say something is fine, most reasonable people will accept you at your word, and think "well great, we can all move on." But when your words don't really match your true feelings, you're essentially expecting others to read your mind. When they fail to magically know what you're REALLY thinking, bubble, bubble, toil and trouble, you end up stirring the cauldron of resentment again, getting more and more angry until you explode over something stupid that isn't the real problem anyway.

It's all about communication and truth. If you find your kitchen looking like a tornado hit it after you've asked your family to clean it up, DO NOT tell them it's "fine" when they offer their inane excuses as to why it's not done. It is not fine, and by telling them it is you've effectively given them permission to blow off anything you ask, because they now know you'll accept their song and dance and do the job yourself.

Similarly, don't let co-workers off the hook with a "fine" when they drop the ball. Scrambling to pick up the pieces someone else should be putting into place does not make you look efficient, it makes you look frantic and unprofessional.

Lastly, if your partner asks you if you're fine and you aren't, don't say that you are. It's a cop-out, it's a waste of time (whatever is bothering you will re-surface in a much uglier way), and it's disrespectful to both of you. Tell the truth if you aren't fine. Talk it out, and if you're not good at that, there's no time like the present to get better at it.

Don't take a perfectly good word like fine and allow it to become your jailer because you use it to let other people take advantage of you. And you are letting them. So this is on you. Don't say something is fine unless it is. If it isn't, make that fact known and don't accept anything less than really, truly fine. Holding people, including yourself, accountable is important, both to your sanity and everyone's personal or professional growth. You're actually doing everyone a favor by withholding "fine" until the job is done correctly. If they don't like you for it, well, that's fine.

Learning and accepting the real meaning of fine is downright liberating. By acknowledging that fine is more than good enough, you'll dial back your daily dose of anxiety to almost manageable levels. And by dispensing fine only when it's deserved, you elevate everyone, including, and especially you.

That is really, truly fine.

Try This!

Think about the last few times you were asked to contribute to or plan a party, a gathering at work or a school event for your children. Was there anything you freaked out about and overdid when "fine" would have done the job? List five things below that you could have scaled back on —and no one would have noticed but you.

1._____

_____

2._____

_____

3._____
_____

4._____
_____

5._____
_____

Next, think about the last few times you told someone something was "fine" when it most definitely was not. Write down the events and then write down what you should have said instead of "it's fine" to change the situation.

_____
_____
_____
_____
_____
_____
_____
_____
_____

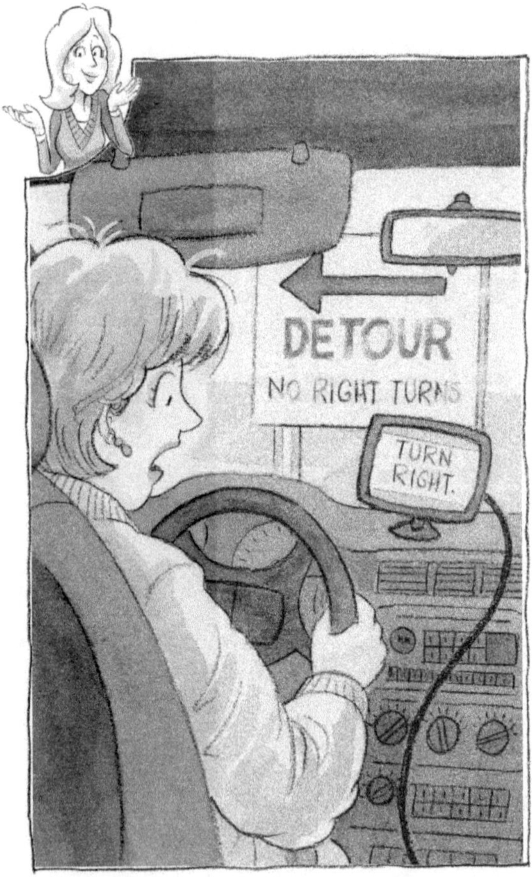
DETOUR
NO RIGHT TURNS
TURN RIGHT.

Chapter 10

Change

Change

verb

1. to make or become different
2. to alter
3. to transform

Oh no you don't.

Pick a woman—any woman who has spent copious amounts of time figuring out how to navigate her life to achieve the fragile balance wherein she manages to: get everyone where they have to be during the day (kids, husband and animals included), handle the increasing needs of aging parents, satisfy the demands of her work life, run a household (remembering to fill up the bathroom soap dispensers and restock the toilet paper because everyone thinks that happens by magic)—and tell her she has to CHANGE.

The word change is more frightening to most women than a forced viewing of *The Exorcist* at home alone on a dark and stormy night with the wind howling and the power going out right after the movie ends. (Sorry, I've seen that damn move a half dozen times and it still scares the crap out of me. Why do I still watch it? No idea.)

Women work ridiculously hard trying to hold everything together for everyone with the complete awareness that the delicate balance we've managed to strike is as unstable as a house of cards, able to be toppled at any moment, with even the most innocuous of changes capable of bringing the whole thing tumbling down.

Change is often forced upon us, and can come in most unwelcome fashion: a job loss, an illness, the end of a relationship. We don't seek those things out. In fact, we hide from them, peeking surreptitiously at changes we know are probably coming, but we don't want to face. Yet, it's not only the big changes that are unwelcome. Small disruptions can be just as unnerving.

For most of us, change equals chaos. As the ones charged with keeping order and executing the daily plan, we could rightfully compare change to one of those nasty Internet viruses. It starts out as a little bug and before you know it, everything is crashing and burning around you.

Change comes at the cost of our control. It amps up the feeling that we're living our lives on the basis of what everyone else needs, which we frequently are. Can you remember the last time you had a day when the only things on your plan were those you wanted/needed to do? Of course you can't; you're a woman, remember?

But routine is comfortable (there's that word again), and when we create a plan and move to complete it, we allow ourselves to perpetuate the illusion that we're in control, that we're calling the shots. As long as nothing changes, we'll manage.

Well, guess what, girls? We aren't calling the shots. At best, we're managing the shots, shots that can change on a dime. And that's what scares us.

Remember the song lyric *"The times, they are a changin'"*? Over the past dozen or so years, the times have changed exponentially, not always for the better. The explosion of the Internet onto the collective consciousness has been a huge blessing—and at times a curse. Enhanced communication and the dissemination of knowledge have not always been used for good, the pivotal example being the terrorist attacks of 2001.

From that point on, the current of anxiety running through society has made us suspicious of any change. Since the larger world frequently seems to be spinning out of control, and we as individuals feel powerless to fix any of it, we hold on even tighter to the stuff we can control. This can make change sound like a really nasty idea, so nasty that even when it's a good idea, we treat it like a bad one.

My husband, God love him, loves to change things. My things, more specifically. Regardless of my idea or plan, and the time it took to develop it, he usually has a better idea. At least he thinks he does. Unfailingly, when I tell him about something I'm going to do, he responds, "Well, what about if you try/do/fix it this way?" at which point I'm yelling and he's running out of the room.

It's not that his ideas are bad, in fact, sometimes they're even good. (If you tell him I said this, I'll deny, deny, deny.) Rather, it's that he's trying to change my plans. The plans I worked so hard to figure out. The plans that have very little to do with what I really want out of my day, but that I'm intent on carrying out because, by god, they're MY PLANS. DO NOT TRY TO CHANGE MY PLANS!

But change, at least the kind we fight against in our daily lives, is really a bogeyman. An imaginary monster that frightens us by the mere idea of its existence, as opposed to any actual harm it does.

Think about it; as a woman, you're already an expert on change. We're called upon to do it our whole lives—so often, in fact, that we fail to realize just how many times we have to make changes in a single day.

Your alarm doesn't go off, making kids late for school and you late for work; the dryer breaks with a full load of wet clothing inside; you forgot to take out something from the freezer for dinner; your mother doesn't feel well and you have to stop in to check on her. Pick a wrench, any wrench, and think about how often it's thrown into the gears of your day.

What do you do? You CHANGE your plan, of course. You just do it. You don't like it, but you do it, because you really don't have any choice. It's annoying, but when you get right down to it, ninety-nine percent of those wrenches aren't that big of a deal. The changes aren't huge; they're more like adjustments or tweaks, and we women are experts at that.

Your skill set includes a heaping helping of tweaking and adjusting. You're good at it. Take a few moments right now to think about how often you have to change your plans and still manage to get everything done. And you do it! Pat yourself on the back and promise to treat yourself to a glass of wine and some chocolate (I say that a lot, don't I? Hmmmm....) later today as a reward, which you'll need because you'll be exhausted from making changes in your plan.

While you're at it, it's time to change the word change. Substitute "adjust" and "tweak." They mean the same thing; they just sound so much more doable and innocent. Then, the next time your plan changes, instead of foaming at the mouth in frustration, take a deep breath and think, *I just need to do a little tweaking; I got this*, because you do, girl, you really do.

But changes to our outward circumstances and plans aren't the only kind of change we dread. Often, it's the deeper stuff, the changes we're asked to make to our beliefs, our values, and our vision of who we really are that can be more personally unnerving.

Any woman with a relationship with another human being knows this. People test us. They test what we think we'll put up with. They test what we think we know about life, love and ourselves. And no one tests us more than our kids.

Before I had children, I was the best mother in the world. I knew how my children would behave; I knew how I would discipline them; I knew how they would grow up.

Then, I actually had them, and all bets were off.

Turns out, I didn't know diddly. Everything I thought I knew, everything I read, everything I thought they would do and then I would do, was wrong, off-base. They did something different, and I was clueless.

So I had to change. Over and over and over again. I had to change my ideas, my behaviors, my expectations—everything. And I hated it. Oh, occasionally, something happened that I didn't expect and it was good, but more often than not, the ka-ka that happened was ka-ka. Huge, steaming piles of it.

So you change because you have to in order to survive, but it ain't easy. It's rarely welcome and often resented. I personally have shaken my fist at the heavens on more than one occasion while ranting, "Really? Really? You couldn't let even ONE THING go my way? I'm so sick of this sh*t!" while those standing close to me step away in anticipation of the lightning strike. (Clearly God is forgiving because it hasn't happened yet. Either that or He/She is adding up all of my transgressions and planning a really big finish. Which I would totally understand.)

Next, throw in the aforementioned exponential changes happening in the world around us. Suddenly, everything about everything has changed overnight. Now it's up to you to relearn how to communicate, how to program the damn television with a remote that could probably fly a plane, how to use a smart phone (which will make you feel really stupid), how to tweet, Instagram, and Pinterest your most fascinating selfies—in short, how to keep from becoming completely and totally irrelevant as the world speeds up and passes you by.

Some days, you feel like you're drowning. It's hopeless; you just don't have the energy to change another thing. You're going to give up…and that's when things start to get interesting. That's when things, and you, start to transform—see definition number three, above.

Change, even (and sometimes especially) forced change, makes us look at things differently.

It can be a kind of cosmic head smack along the lines of, "Wake up! It's time to do something new!" When things don't go as planned, we have no choice but to alter course, which can lead to unanticipated blessings and experiences.

Before there was *Not Ready for Granny Panties*, there was just me, working as a newspaper columnist for a number of papers in Philadelphia and the surrounding areas. With the explosion of the Internet, my newspapers changed course or simply disappeared, one by one, until I was left with…well, not much. It was a seismic change, and one that, let's be honest—sucked.

I had no choice. I had to change, which, for me, meant learning about and embracing the Internet. I taught myself how to blog, creating not only *Not Ready for Granny Panties*, but also other websites for myself and then for others. I learned how to make mini movies, edit photos, create a YouTube channel, embed content, share content, and ultimately find an audience that brought me readers from around the globe.

I began speaking to women about getting older (Ugh!) and how to live vital, joyful lives in spite of the numbers. I created webinars, workshops and classes, meeting interesting, wonderful women who shared my slightly off-beat sense of humor and mindset. In the process, I also found some fantastic women (Chrysa Smith, Pat Achilles, and Carmen Ferriero-Esteban), who joined me on *NRFGP*, becoming friends whom I cherish.

To say it's been challenging is an understatement. And there are things about the whole thing which I kind of hate (social media, anyone?). But the forced change has transformed me, my writing, my audience, and pretty much everything else about what I do and how I do it.

Has it all been a blessing? Oh come on. I was *comfortable* where I was. Change is most definitely *uncomfortable*, at least for a while. And sure, there are days when I'd chuck it all to go back to writing my little columns and hitting "send" without a second thought. (Those tend to be the days when I have to tweet something or otherwise engage in mindless blather through social media. But I'm not complaining. Okay, maybe just a little.) All in all, it's been an amazing experience, one I'd never have had if left to my own devices and choices.

It's important to be flexible when it comes to seismic changes. They're often so powerful that you can't prepare for them, which makes it even more necessary to be ready to go with the flow and open to new possibilities when they arrive. However, the way you handle even small changes—or tweaks or adjustments—that you face on any given day can make a difference in your life and outlook.

Sometimes it helps to use what I call the 10-10-10 rule. (I think I first heard about this from Oprah, to give credit where due.) Whenever a forced change comes your way, whether it be the loss of a job or a traffic jam that keeps you from getting dinner on the table on time, put the change up against the 10-10-10 rule. How important will this be in 10 minutes, 10 months and 10 years? Usually, a little perspective is all it takes to tweak your attitude enough to blow off the change (really, a bowl of cereal for dinner never killed anyone), or face it in a positive way. (Maybe now that my job is changing, I can think about my dream of doing _____.)

Change has a way of igniting us. Usually, it's mixed with fear, but if we embrace it and perhaps institute it on our own, even in the smallest of ways, we can de-demonize it and recognize its transformative powers. (Try a new lipstick or nail color, maybe doing a 180 from your usual. I'm generally a pink and coral kind of girl, but I tried this blue polish on my toes and I'm loving it!) We'll see things differently, we'll see ourselves differently, and maybe we'll start to behave differently, opening new doors in the process.

So really, the best change of all is a change of attitude. Change is gonna happen anyway, so why not get a jump on it? And in the process, you might just change your life—for the better.

Try This!

Think about the last major change you experienced and write about it below. Was it a "forced" change?

What seemed bad about it? What seemed good? How could you have looked at it differently?

_____

_____

_____

_____

Now, think of some small changes you could institute in your life, perhaps in different areas—your wardrobe, your work, your home life. Write down at least five changes below. Next to each, write what you hope will happen when you make the changes.

1._____

_____

2._____

_____

3._____

_____

4._____

_____

5._____

_____

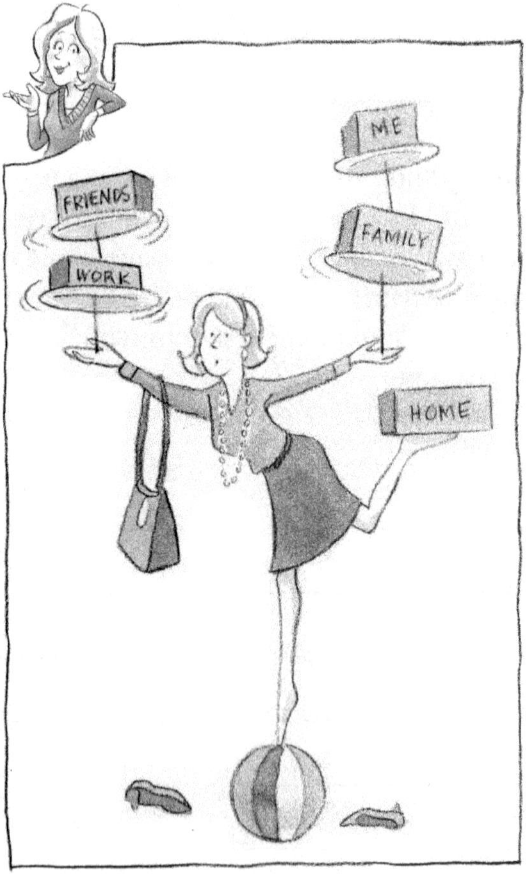
ME
FRIENDS
FAMILY
WORK
HOME

Chapter 11

Balance

Bal·ance

verb

1. to evenly distribute weight

noun

2. a state of equilibrium
3. equal stability between two opposing sides

"I can bring home the bacon, fry it up in a pan, and never let you forget you're a man! 'Cause I'm a woooooooman!"

No, that's not what I sing to my husband every day. It's a line from a classic—and by classic I mean hilarious—'80's commercial for a perfume.

In the ad, a well-dressed, attractive woman alternately appears in business attire holding a briefcase, in khakis holding a frying pan and in a slinky, low-cut evening gown tossing her hair back and forth as the ditty above plays in the background.

As the ad implies, she can do it all, and smell really good in the process.

That's some perfume.

It's also a load of crap, at least if you think you can do it all and end your day in a slinky, low-cut evening gown with nary a hair out of place.

Yet, that's the fairy tale women were sold as more and more of us entered the workforce full time, while trying to raise families. Work full time and raise a family, while also trying to keep a home from turning into a hazardous waste dump, care for aging parents, maintain friendships, grocery shop, bake cupcakes for the school party, get the dog to the vet, pick up the dry cleaning, and remember your spouse or significant other's name. Simultaneously. At the same time. All at once.

We toss our hair, all right, but it's usually when we're banging our heads against a wall.

I won't go so far as to say it can't be done. It's done all the time, by women who should be sporting Wonder Woman undies beneath their clothes. (They really do make them; I bought several pairs at Target. I wear them regularly.)

But I daresay that if you asked any one of the women doing it all, they'd admit that they don't do it all well, at least not everything every day. Without several clones running around picking up the slack—or the dry cleaning—stuff is gonna fall through the cracks. It's inevitable.

Which is why the word balance is kind of a joke.

By its definition, balance requires equality. Equal weight has to be given to both sides of the scale for things to truly balance. Just how often does that happen in your life?

Think about it: You have an important presentation at work in the morning. You get up a few minutes early, get dressed, greet your family, hand off everyone's lunch and shoo everybody out the door. You're just about to grab your briefcase and leave the house when one of the kids bursts back inside and says, a) "We missed the bus!" if your kids are still in school, or b) "My car won't start and I have to get to work!" if your kids are employed.

The details are irrelevant. What matters is that once again, your work-life balance (who came up with that euphemism?) is decidedly out of balance. Because now, even though if you get involved you'll be late and you really should tell everyone to figure it out for themselves, you won't. You're the mom. You're the woman. That's not what we do.

So you herd yourself and whomever you're driving into your car and get them to school or work on time, which means that you are not. On time, that is.

Or consider this: You've been trying to get a meeting with an important client for months. Conflicting schedules force you to set up an evening meeting, which you set in stone; you really need to keep these people happy. At dinner with your family that evening, a) your son tells you his team made the playoffs and the game is the same time as your meeting or b) your husband surprises you with concert tickets—on the night of your appointment.

Once more, the details are irrelevant. Regardless of what you decide to do, someone will be hurt, disappointed, or possibly annoyed enough to cancel their account with you. Any way you look at it, you lose. And so does the work-life balance. Again.

The term "work-life balance" should be used in conjunction with another word—guilt. Because every time a woman fails to maintain balance in her life, she feels guilty. She feels like she's failed. Failed her family, failed her employer, failed herself. And by the way, has anyone noticed that no one asks men how they're doing with their work-life balance?

I'll happily give men their due as having evolved with a more hands-on approach to child care. Many men today (my son, now a new father, included), are only too happy to pitch in with the kids, changing diapers, running them to practices and games, even doing the occasional load of laundry. And that's great, but isn't that what parents are supposed to do? Again, give the guys their due, but I'm not sure anyone deserves a trophy for taking on some of the responsibilities of parenting. If they do, then women should be canonized, crowned, and immortalized in song. Which doesn't happen, because it's *our job* to take care of the kids. When the guys help out, we're not supposed to expect it; we're supposed to be grateful.

Plus, if there is a conflict of work schedules between parents and something's gotta give, usually, it's the woman's work that takes a back seat. I'm not pointing fingers; it's just the way it is. Men aren't expected to maintain a work-life balance. They're expected to work, and if they do any of the other stuff, it's above and beyond the call of duty, noteworthy and applause-worthy.

Lest you think it's only women with young children who struggle, let me assure you, the saying, "Little kids, little problems, big kids, big problems" is true. Even if your kids are chronologically adults, you're not off the hook. And should you be caring for grandchildren so your own children can go to work, you know firsthand that taking care of your kids doesn't stop when they turn eighteen. In fact, it often just gets more complicated and demanding.

The fact that most women have to work today in order to help support a family, essentially holding down two full-time jobs—one at work and one at home—has little effect on the expectation that we should be able to get everything accomplished all of the time. Yet, I could cite study after study that notes how challenging, if not impossible, it is to work full-time and run a household without things imploding occasionally. However, there's an easier way to prove it—do the math.

There are twenty-four hours in a day. Setting aside a conservative eight to eleven hours for sleeping, eating and personal care, then subtracting eight for the workday, you're left with eight or fewer hours to get to and from work, get meals prepared, oversee homework, take everyone to practices, games or lessons, handle errands like grocery shopping and getting the car inspected, clean the house, do the laundry, schedule and attend doctor and dentist appointments, and manage the unexpected, like the washing machine going on the fritz. Oh, and don't forget calling your mother, buying that gift for the bridal shower you were invited to, and paying your bills.

Do I need to go on? Simply put, on any given day, there are just not enough hours to get everything done, let alone maintain any kind of balance.

Trying to achieve perfect balance is a precarious business. Think Nik Wallenda walking on a tightrope across Niagara Falls. One misstep and you're history. Okay, maybe you're not likely to be hurled to your death in a raging torrent of water, but when the balance scale tips, the delicate scaffolding you've erected to keep your life functioning can fold like the little pig's house of straw. It often does, leading to not only the collapse of your plan, but a gnawing anxiety over your "failure."

But how much have you really failed? If you look unflinchingly at everything you're trying to balance, is it really so tragic if you just don't do it all every day?

Take a moment and think—really think—about the last time you messed up on your work-life balance. Did anyone die? Did you lose your house? What actually happened that was so awful, besides, of course, what you did to yourself when you "failed?" Probably nothing. Nothing with lasting consequences, that is. Maybe you missed a meeting or a deadline. Maybe someone didn't get wherever they were supposed to be on time. Maybe someone even got mad at you for a while. (Horror of horrors!) I'm willing to bet that whatever the consequences, everyone got over it. (And if someone being mad at you for a while means they leave you alone and don't ask you for anything, is that really such a bad thing?)

Everyone has "stuff." Stuff that takes attention off of what we might want to be doing at any given time. Stuff that keeps us from accomplishing what we want to accomplish. But that stuff is precisely what provides the balance between us and everyone else.

During some of my darkest days, mainly when dealing with my son's former addiction issues, my life was unbalanced. Actually, that's an understatement. It was a train wreck. For a long time, I hid what was going on for a lot of reasons, one of which was that I couldn't let go of the idea that somehow all of it was my fault and therefore I had no excuses for my daily failures. But a funny thing happened when I started to share, even in minor ways, what was happening in my life. People understood. They cut me a break, which allowed me to cut myself a break.

I began to see that if I didn't get something done or I fell behind on a project, it was okay. I needed that energy for survival, and the other things could wait. Balance wasn't important, because when you're dealing with a raging, out-of-his mind drug addict, there simply is no balance to be had.

The next time you have stuff, or even if you just forget to do something, admit it. Tell whoever needs to know that you goofed. I'm willing to bet that not only will you be forgiven, you'll discover a comradery with others who are relieved to know they aren't the only ones dropping the ball. And voila—the scale slowly tips back in the direction of balance—and forgiveness, which is even more important, especially if you can forgive yourself.

Ultimately, balance is a myth, kind of like unicorns and fairies. We'd love to believe, but no one's actually seen it, and we still feel lousy when we drop the work-life balance ball. So here's my suggestion: Don't just drop the ball, heave it as forcefully and far away from you as possible.

The only balance you need to achieve is that which keeps you upright when you put two feet on the ground in the morning and get out of bed. After that, it's all open to interpretation.

Interpretation of what? Whatever is going on in your day. Some days, that's going to mean work is a priority. Some days, family will be where you need to spend the bulk of your energy. And still other days, you get to be the key variable in the equation and be your own priority for a change.

Balance is fluid, not stationary. Some days it requires focus in one area, some days another. And sometimes, it's more than days, it can be weeks or even months when the scales are tipped in one direction or another. And that's okay.

What's not okay is holding yourself to impossible standards. You cannot bring home the bacon, fry it up in a pan, and never let him forget he's a man, at least not every single day. As for the evening gown and perfect hair, most of us would settle for not having lipstick on our teeth, finding a pair of tights or panty hose without a run in them in our drawer, and not having to tweeze chin hair.

It's all about perspective. But if the idea of achieving balance still floats your boat, think of it in little-picture/big-picture ways.

When you start hyperventilating because your life is out of balance, stop what you're doing and take a breath. Pull out the 10-10-10 rule again and ask yourself if whatever you're involved in will matter 10 minutes, 10 months, or 10 years from now. Then apply the same standard to whatever you feel is out of balance in your life at the moment. Don't be afraid to tweak the moment to make an adjustment, letting something go if necessary and possibly restoring a sense of balance, if only momentarily.

Later, when you've locked yourself in the bathroom for ten minutes (and yes, every woman should do so at least once daily), step back and look at the bigger picture. If you find that a quick evaluation (it doesn't take more than that—you know when you're listing to one side) indicates that things are seriously out of whack, decide one of two things: how you can make an adjustment or how you can let yourself off the hook and deal with whatever demand life is making on you until things even out a bit—without beating yourself up because your life isn't balanced.

Finally, stop evaluating yourself based on anyone else's idea of what your life should be. It's your life, and your balance is unique to you, no one else. Leave the tightrope walking to Nik Wallenda. Think of your own personal balance as more of a Macy's Thanksgiving parade balloon—held down by multiple ropes and constantly shifting gently with the wind to stay afloat.

And never mind the bacon; it's not good for you anyway.

Try This!

Think about your week ahead. Write down ten things you have to accomplish, including both work-related and personal items. Next to each, prioritize them as A, B, or C tasks. Finally, notice if your "balance" is skewed. Recognize that balance is an illusion and will change not only weekly, but daily!

1. _____
2. _____
3. _____
4. _____
5. _____
6. _____
7. _____
8. _____
9. _____
10. _____

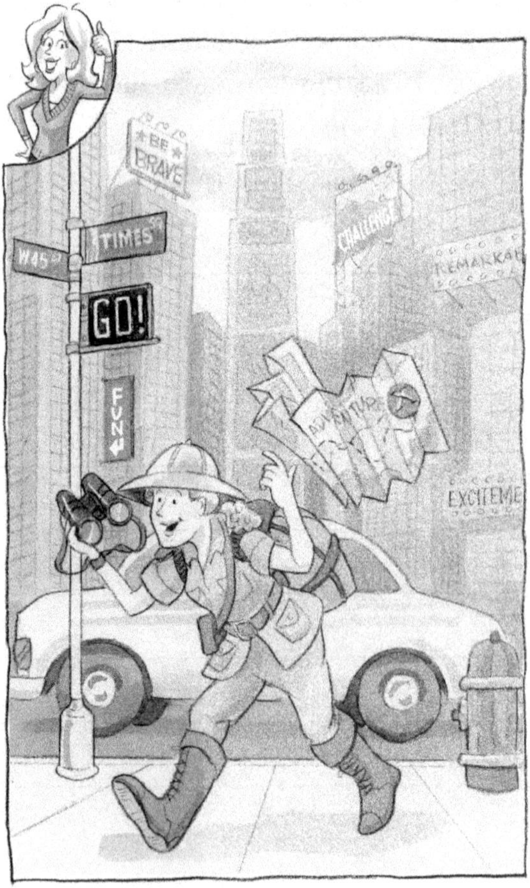
BE
BRAVE
W 45
TIMES
GO!
FUN

Chapter 12

Adventure

Ad·ven·ture

noun

1. an exciting or dangerous experience.
2. a risky undertaking
3. an unusual, remarkable experience with an unknown outcome

Let me think.... When was the last time I had an adventure?

That is, aside from the time last week when I spent twenty minutes wandering the grocery store aisles in search of the peanut butter, which they moved *again*.

That was exciting, but nothing compared to the four months when they were remodeling the entire grocery store and no one could find anything. Weekly food shopping took so long people were tearing through bags of chips in the aisles for sustenance and snarling with bared teeth at anyone who dared question them. Not that I ever did that, but to this day, I can't look at a bag of Doritos without breaking out in a sweat and frantically searching for a map.

A treasure hunt in the grocery store: not exactly a romp through the jungle wearing a pith helmet in search of an elusive Bengal tiger. But for most of us, it's more than enough.

"Adventure" is a scary word for women. Just look at the words used to define it: "dangerous, risky, unusual, remarkable, unknown."

Seriously? How many women do you know look at those words and say, "Yeah, I gotta get me some of that!"? Most women not only avoid all things risky and dangerous in their own lives, but do everything in their power to squash it in the lives of those closest to them.

Without getting too anthropological, our avoidance of adventure goes back a long way. In the days of spears and hunting for dinner, we gals were busy picking berries and leaves for the early version of a spinach salad with craisins, while the guys were out playing hide and seek with growling things sporting claws and fangs. For women, a pounding pulse and an adrenalin rush usually meant you'd better run, or instead of preparing dinner, there was a good chance you would BE dinner.

Now think for a moment about the words "unusual and unknown." Did the hair on your neck stand up just a little? Unusual and unknown mean you'll probably have to CHANGE something. Your plan isn't going to work. Stuff is going to happen that you don't know how to handle. And we already discussed how we feel about that.

None of us is being hunted by tigers. But that doesn't keep us from feeling panicked when something unknown gets tossed in our direction. Anything that makes our pulse pound or gives us an adrenalin rush sends us sprinting towards the medicine cabinet to down a few aspirin and then to the computer to look up the symptoms of a heart attack. Of course, that's what's happening, because what could be good about a pounding pulse?

Actually, plenty.

Since we're pulling words out of the definition, let's look at a few others, namely, "exciting" and "remarkable."

When was the last time you described something as "remarkable?"

For me, it was a few weeks ago, when I met friends Chrysa and Carmen for lunch at the Comcast building in Philadelphia. After waiting around twenty minutes for clearance to get in (it's a communications company, but the computers weren't working), we rode an express elevator to the forty-third floor to a restaurant which serves as the cafeteria for employees. Yes, the food was good, but it was the view that was truly remarkable.

Like other children growing up, I learned the requisite lessons on local geography when I was in school. So I sort of remembered that Philadelphia is bounded by two rivers, the Delaware and the Schuylkill (don't even try to figure out how to say it —it's impossible). But squiggly lines on a flat map leave little impression. Yet up there, looking through floor-to-ceiling windows, *I could see them.* I could see both rivers, stretching and winding around the city, cupping it on either side, life teeming in between with no notice of the extraordinary landscape. It was remarkable. (My general feelings about Comcast can be summed up in a blog post I wrote for *Not Ready for Granny Panties* titled, "Comcast—The Tenth Circle of Hell," but they do have a really nice restaurant.)

It was also an adventure, one which I never thought would deserve the title when I half-heartedly rifled through my closet for something to wear that morning. *So, we'll go in town and have lunch*, I thought. *It'll be nice.* It was more than nice; it was exciting, breathtaking.

That's the thing about adventures. We tend to think of them as grand, overwrought experiences, full of things that instinctively cause us to shrink away. Full of things that scare us. Truth be told, I was a little scared, having a fear of heights and falling and all that stuff. So my pulse did quicken a bit, which was actually kind of cool.

We also think of adventures as things that are beyond the realm of the possible for us in our frequently mundane, everyday lives. Which is exactly why this adventure was so wonderful. This adventure grew out of an ordinary experience—having lunch, which is not only not very scary, but something we all do every single day.

So let's redefine our concept of adventure. Instead of assuming an adventure must involve a predator, a flight to a remote tropical jungle, and/or quicksand, let's consider the possibility that an adventure could be as close as an ordinary meal.

In fact, a meal is a great place to dip your toe into the world of adventure. I'll venture to guess that when you decide to eat out, several things happen:

- You eat at one of two or three favorite places
- You order one of two or three favorite things
- You sit in the exact same spot because your husband has some weird attachment to the two stools at the end of the bar and he has a meltdown if anyone else is sitting there

Okay, maybe that last one just pertains to me and Dave. (Really, a few weeks ago we had to sit a few seats away from where we usually sit at Bertucci's and I thought he was going to have a panic attack.) But you get the idea. When we get to a certain point, comfortable (there's that nasty word again) takes precedence over everything else.

Which I get, most of the time. But every once in a while, is trying something different such a bad idea?

I'm willing to bet that wherever you live, there's a restaurant somewhere nearby that features cuisine you're unfamiliar with. Indian food, Thai food, even Japanese food (and no, it's not exactly the same as Chinese food). A food adventure will not only treat your taste buds to something they don't expect, but the atmosphere will likely transport you to a foreign locale right in your own neighborhood. (And hokey as it may seem, those Japanese chefs really do amazing things with knives.)

Adventures can be personal in scale, too. When's the last time you tried a new hair style or color? Every woman knows that a good hair day is usually a good day. But a new 'do can work wonders on your attitude. It can change the way you see yourself and the way others see you, which can boost your confidence. This can indirectly lead to new opportunities or the courage to take on something that's been just waiting for you to say, "Yes!"

Looking for something grander? No need to renew your passport and hop a plane—of course, if you can do so, go for it. Instead, think for a moment. What's near you? Are you a suburbanite? Why not venture into the nearest city and explore a museum, see a show, learn some history? In Philadelphia, the diversity offered by the rich cultures of neighborhoods can take you to the Italian Market or Chinatown for foreign flavors, the educational mecca of University

City, or the richly historical Old City, each area offering its own charms and adventures.

Conversely, if you're a city dweller, when's the last time you saw some wide-open spaces? Letting nature take the lead can offer an adventure in perspective and wonder. Have you ever gone fishing? The first time you feel the tug of a live creature on a line is incredible. Even walking in an unfamiliar natural environment spells adventure. On a recent visit to Florida, my daughter and I were entertained on a nature walk by hundreds of weird little crabs with one giant claw and one tiny one that scurried around a marsh. Like something out of a science fiction movie, but also very cool.

Are any of these things going to make your pulse pound? Perhaps not pound, at least not at first. Your beginning adventures will likely quicken your pulse, which is enough early on. Because once you start having adventures, even small ones, you'll realize they aren't so scary after all. You'll want more. This is easy enough to accomplish when you finally do start saying, "Yes" to the opportunities that wait right outside of your door.

My friend, Lu Ann Cahn, a really amazing woman and long-time Philadelphia news reporter, illustrates this idea beautifully in her book, *I Dare Me*. Finding herself in a life-slump, Lu Ann decided to challenge herself to do one new thing every day for an entire year. Sometimes, her "dares" were silly —walk backwards for a day—sometimes fun—

learn to hula hoop—and sometimes really daring—take the "Polar Plunge" and run into the ocean with a bunch of other lunatics in January. Yet regardless of what she decided to do on any given day, she realized that by saying, "Yes" to new things, she was crafting a new adventure for herself every single day.

The dares led to adventures, which led to amazing experiences, which led to opportunities, which led to a new attitude—perhaps the most important development of the entire experiment. By saying, "Yes," Lu Ann found adventure, redefined her life and had FUN.

You can, too.

Start small—silly, even—or take on something bigger. It really doesn't matter. What does matter is what cultivating an adventurous spirit will mean for your life: life-changing experiences, opportunities and empowerment.

And who knows? Maybe there's a pith helmet and a tropical jungle in your future after all.

Try This!

When was the last time you had an adventure? How did it make you feel? Write about the experience below.

_____

_____

_____

_____

_____

_____

Now, list five adventures you'd like to have. Be sure to include at least one thing you feel may be totally out of reach. Next to each, write down one thing you could do to make your adventure a reality.

1._____

_____

2._____

_____

3._____

_____

4._____

_____

5._____

_____

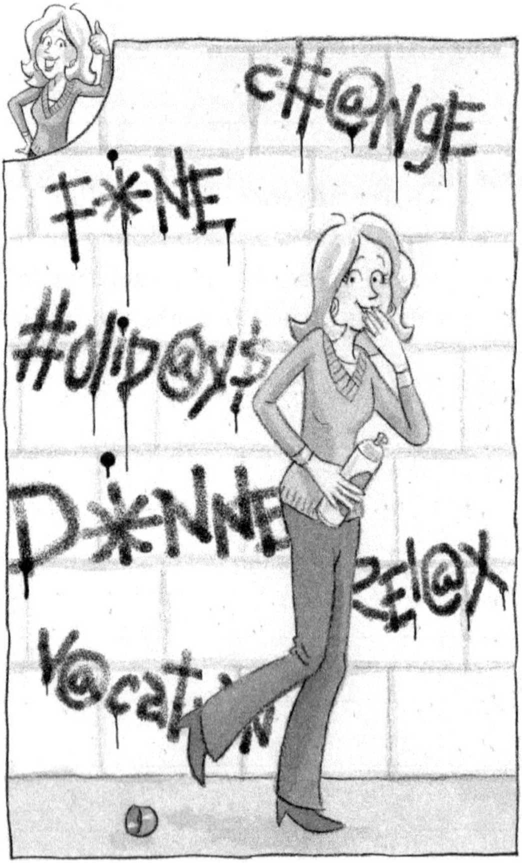
c#@ngE
F*NE
#olid@y$
REl@x

Chapter 13

Epilogue

Ep·i·logue

noun

1. a conclusion or summary at the end of a book or play
2. the end

What's in a word? As it turns out, plenty. And when you're tossing out nearly 20,000 of them every day, it's a pretty safe bet that some will get you into trouble.

But as we've seen, a word doesn't have to be intrinsically terrifying to strike fear into the heart of a woman. In fact, the words that frequently fill us with fear and loathing are often the very words that send everyone else to their happy place.

Who doesn't love a vacation, a tasty dinner or a holiday? A lot of women, if we're being honest. While we can easily get on board with the idea of any of the above, and we have, when our own mothers were doing the work to pull them off, now that we're in the driver's seat, vacations, dinners, and holidays most often mean work, work, and more work.

But with a little tweaking, we can redefine what those words mean, adjusting everyone's expectations—especially our own—and perhaps remember what it feels like to get juiced by the thought of vacations, dinners, and holidays, instead of breaking out in a cold sweat and hyperventilating at the mere mention of the words.

Before we can do that, though, a little more aversion therapy is in order. It's time to get over our fear of the word, "No," to stop worrying about being nice, and to recognize that fine is absolutely fine. Anyone who doesn't agree is free to create their own definitions elsewhere.

We also need to relax (without getting too comfortable), embrace change and find a balance that works for us. Or just forget about balance altogether and let the chips fall where they may, which is pretty much all we can do anyway.

Are you overwhelmed? Don't be. Everything we've talked about can be summed up in a phrase: LIGHTEN UP. Lighten up on yourself. Lighten up on those around you. Play a game of "I don't give a damn" every once in a while. When you do, you'll find that more often than you can imagine, what you were giving a damn about wasn't really worth the angst in the first place.

It's okay to let go of the words that send you over the edge. They're just words. The only power they have is what we give them, and take away from them. So take some of it away already. If serving everyone Cheerios for dinner some night when you're just exhausted works, do it. Do you know how many people would give anything for a bowl of Cheerios and milk?

Perfect is overrated. In fact, it's most often in moments of imperfection that the best memories are made. Do you know how in the movie, *The Christmas Story*, the family has to eat Christmas dinner at a Chinese restaurant after the neighbor's dogs destroy their feast and they end up being serenaded by Chinese waiters while the restaurant owner chops the head off a duck right at the table? It's hilarious, and as recounted by the narrator, the most memorable Christmas dinner ever. And okay, it's a movie, but think back to your most memorable experiences. I'm willing to bet that more than a few of them involved things veering off track, sometimes spectacularly, which is exactly what makes the occasion memorable. (One of our most memorable occasions occurred when our water heater sprung a leak in the middle of a party. We called the repairman, who fixed the heater then joined us for dinner.)

Perfect is also a synonym for failure, for the simple reason that it's impossible to achieve. So what exactly are you trying to do to yourself by allowing words to run your life?

Given that we ladies talk so much, it's time to do some talking to ourselves. Remind yourself that life is what you make it. I don't believe that we control everything that happens to us (if the Universe gives you what you want, where's my winning Powerball ticket?). But I do believe that our response to whatever is going on is all within our control and can influence not only how we feel about things, but how we respond to them, which in turn affects everything.

So while you will still be responsible for running the asylum, you don't have to be a prison warden about it. Lighten up on absolutely everything, which will not only give you some room to breathe, as well as to rediscover your own happy places, it will force everyone else to be just a bit more responsible for their own lives, happiness and occasionally, dinner. While that may cause some temporary angst among the troops, eventually everyone wins, especially if the goal is to get everyone out of the house and living independently of you before you need an oxygen tank and a walker.

Finally, once you've adjusted and redefined and just lightened up, you'll be ready for an adventure. And whether that's a month in Italy or a trip to a local restaurant serving Moroccan cuisine, you'll get your juices flowing. You might even get excited and have FUN. Remember fun?

If you take nothing else away from this, do take "fun" off of your dirty words list. It's a powerful thing, this fun. You're entitled to it; you deserve it. And when you free yourself from your list of dirty words, you'll be surprised to find opportunities for fun exist almost everywhere. (Okay, maybe not at the gynecologist or the dentist, but still.)

If you're a woman, you're going to talk. So say the right things. Take back the words that used to make you happy. Talk yourself into joy and living your best life (thank you, Oprah) every day. Sure, some days will be better than others, but with a new dictionary in your head, every day has potential for joy. Claim it; own it and live it.

Before long, the only dirty words you'll recall will be the four-letter ones, which, of course, can be quite useful in their own right. And that's exactly as it should be.

ABOUT THE AUTHOR

MARY FRAN BONTEMPO is an award winning author, speaker, humorist, and teacher who writes for and about women. After surviving the perfect storm—loss of work, a child suffering from addiction, and turning fifty—Mary Fran learned that a sense of humor and honesty about some really crappy stuff could help a gal get through the muck. *Not Ready for Granny Panties*, the blog, was born, followed by *The 11 Commandments for Avoiding Granny Panties*, published in 2012. Her first book, *Everyday Adventures or, As My Husband Says, "Lies, Lies and More Lies,"* was published in 2007. Mary Fran speaks frequently to women's groups about aging (Ugh!) and finding laughter in life's middle ground. Her work has been honored by the Erma Bombeck Writer's Workshop and Humor Press, among others. She currently writes for her blog, (www.notreadyforgrannypanties.com), and *Women's Voices Magazine*. Visit Mary Fran at http://www.maryfranbontempo.com.

ABOUT THE ILLUSTRATOR

PAT ACHILLES is, in her own words, the anti-artist: too chubby to be edgy, too realistic to be abstract, and too easily distracted to be intense. Pat infuses her drawings with fun and hasn't found a subject she can't illustrate with skill and humor, including theatrical posters, caricatures, children's books, logos, custom cards, and more. To see more of Pat's work, go to www.achillesportfolio.com.

ACKNOWLEDGEMENTS

In addition to my wonderful family, there are my soul sisters to thank, for without their inspiration, there would be no book, and no me, as I am today.

So, thank you to my mom, Ann Dettra; my real sister, Karen Fisher; my sister-in-law, Dianna Dettra; my niece, Kate; the Bontempo women; Chrysa Smith; Pat Achilles; my BFF, Chris Cherwien; my college BFF, Donna Armstrong; my bikini-wearing bitches—Lee Anne Englert, Jennifer Gardella and Denice Whiteley; my hero, Kathy Harold; my "almost" cousin, Gina Furia Rubel; Brenda Krueger Huffman; Sara Canuso; Joey Fortman; Lynn Doyle; Jamie Broderick and the Network Now family; my grade school girlfriends; Ellen Faulkner; Lynnis Woods-Mullins; Jill Hickey; my wonderful editor, Laurel Garver; and Dorothy Gale, who, since I was a little girl, has always inspired me to look over the rainbow.